AAT

TECHNICIAN
NVQ AND DIPLOMA PATHWAY
(DIPLOMA)

REVISION **COMPANION**   Unit 11

Drafting Financial
Statements
(Accounting Practice,
Industry and Commerce)

For exams in
December 2008 and
June 2009

BPP

LEARNING MEDIA

Sixth edition April 2008
First edition 2002

ISBN 9780 7517 4636 5 (previous edition 0 7517 3232 0)

British Library Cataloguing-in-Publication Data
A catalogue record for this book is available from the British Library

Published by

BPP Learning Media Ltd,
BPP House,
Aldine Place,
London, W12 8AA

www.bpp.com/learningmedia

Printed in Great Britain by
Martins of Berwick
Sea View Works
Spittal
Berwick-upon-Tweed
TD15 1RS

We are grateful to the AAT for permission to reproduce specimen
assessments and examples from previous exam based assessments.   All
answers have been prepared by BPP Learning Media Ltd.

CONTENTS

Introduction (v)

Chapter activities	Questions	Answers
1 Introduction to financial statements	1	125
2 Introduction to limited companies	5	131
3 Published financial statements of limited companies	7	135
4 Reporting financial performance	21	151
5 The cash flow statement	23	155
6 Non-current assets	33	165
7 Inventories, taxation, provisions and events after the balance sheet date	37	171
8 Further accounting standards	41	177
9 Interpreting financial statements	43	179
10 The consolidated balance sheet	55	195
11 Group accounts – further aspects	63	207

Practice exam based assessments

	Questions	Answers
Practice exam based assessment 1: Haydn plc	67	211
Practice exam based assessment 2: Trustdan plc	77	223
Practice exam based assessment 3: Howardsend Ltd	89	235
Practice exam based assessment 4: Ricschtein Ltd	99	247
Practice exam based assessment 5: Benard Ltd	111	255
Proforma forms		267

INTRODUCTION

This is BPP Learning Media's Revision Companion for Unit 11, Drafting Financial Statements. It is part of an integrated package of AAT materials.

It has been written in conjunction with the BPP Course Companion and has been carefully designed to enable students to practise all aspects of the requirements of the Standards of Competence and performance criteria. It is fully up to date as at April 2008 and reflects the Standards of Competence and the exams set to date.

This Revision Companion contains these key features:

- graded activities corresponding to each chapter of the Course Companion
- a selection of the AAT's exams for Unit 11 up to and including December 2007.

The emphasis in all activities and questions is on the practical application of the skills acquired.

Tutors adopting our Companions (minimum of ten Course Companions and ten Revision Companions per Unit, or ten Combined Companions as appropriate) are entitled to free access to the Lecturers' Area resources, including the Tutor Companion. To obtain your log-in, e-mail lecturersvc@bpp.com.

Home Study students are also entitled to access to additional resources. You will have received your log-in details on registration.

If you have any comments about this book, please e-mail pippariley@bpp.com or write to Pippa Riley, Publishing Projects Director, BPP Learning Media Ltd, BPP House, Aldine Place, London W12 8AA.

Note: Diploma Pathway

This book is suitable for all students preparing for AAT Unit 11, both NVQ and Diploma Pathway.

Proforma forms

In your Unit 11 exam you will probably be supplied with proformas of the key documents that you will be asked to produce. We include a copy of these forms at the back of this book for you to photocopy and use when practising the relevant activities.

chapter 1:
INTRODUCTION TO FINANCIAL STATEMENTS

1 What type of general information will the following users of financial statements require?

i) Investors
ii) Loan creditors
iii) Employees
iv) Management

2 What are the main differences between a sole trader and a limited company?

3 Explain what is meant by:

i) relevant information
ii) reliable information

4 Fill in the gaps.

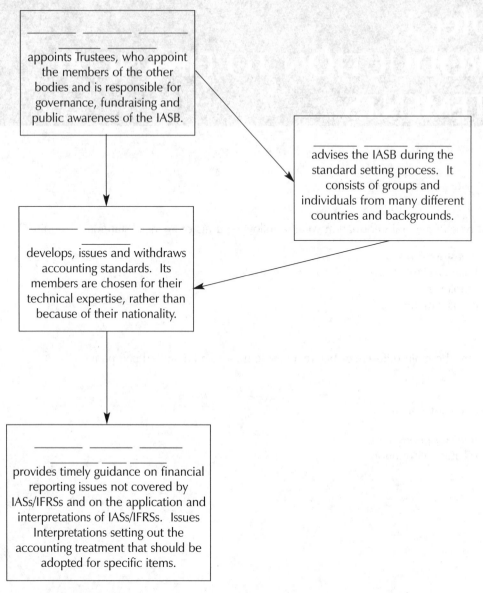

_____ _____ - _____ _____

appoints Trustees, who appoint the members of the other bodies and is responsible for governance, fundraising and public awareness of the IASB.

_____ _____ _____

advises the IASB during the standard setting process. It consists of groups and individuals from many different countries and backgrounds.

_____ _____ - _____ _____

develops, issues and withdraws accounting standards. Its members are chosen for their technical expertise, rather than because of their nationality.

_____ - _____ _____ - _____ _____ ____ _____

provides timely guidance on financial reporting issues not covered by IASs/IFRSs and on the application and interpretations of IASs/IFRSs. Issues Interpretations setting out the accounting treatment that should be adopted for specific items.

5 What are the objectives of the IASB?

6 What are the main purposes of the Framework for the Preparation and Presentation of Financial Statements?

7 In a set of financial statements all assets are stated at their original cost to the business. Of which accounting concept is this an example?

8 Describe each of the following accounting concepts and give an example of how each affects the figures that appear in a set of financial statements.

  i)   Accruals
  ii)   Going concern
  iii) Consistency
  iv)   Prudence
  v)   Materiality
  vi)   Money measurement

9 What are the IASB Framework definitions of the following elements of financial statements?

  i)   Asset
  ii)   Liability
  iii) Income
  iv)   Expenses

10 Complete the following two versions of the accounting equation using the terms for the elements of financial statements from the IASB Framework.

  i)   Assets – liabilities   = ...

  ii) Equity   = Contributions from owners + ...

                                 – .... – ....

11 Give three examples of users of financial statements outside a company, other than the shareholders, who may be interested in its financial statements. For each user, state what purpose they would use them for.

chapter 2:
INTRODUCTION TO LIMITED COMPANIES

1 Briefly explain each of the following terms:

   i)   Separate legal personality
   ii)   Limited liability
   iii) Ordinary shares
   iv)   Preference shares
   v)   Directors

2 What are the advantages and disadvantages of trading as a limited company?

3 Are each of the following reserves distributable or non-distributable? Complete the table.

	Distributable	Non-distributable
Revaluation reserve		
Retained earnings reserve		
Share premium account		
Plant replacement reserve		
General reserve		

4 What are debentures? Compare debentures to ordinary share capital.

5 When Pegasus Ltd was first set up on 1 January 20X0 the authorised share capital was made up of 500,000 50 pence ordinary shares. On that date 100,000 shares were issued for £0.80 each. On 1 January 20X1 the directors made a 1 for 5 bonus issue of shares. On 31 December 20X1 the directors made a 1 for 4 rights issue at a price of £1.00 per share.

Show the journal entries required for each of the following events:

i)   1 January 20X0 – issue of shares
ii)   1 January 20X1 – bonus issue
iii)   31 December 20X1 – rights issue.

6   Given below is the trial balance of Unicorn Ltd at 31 March 20X2.

	£	£
Ordinary share capital (£1 ordinary shares)		100,000
Share premium		50,000
Sales		940,000
Purchases	564,000	
Inventory at 1 April 20X1	47,000	
Trade receivables and payables	156,000	141,000
Prepayments and accruals	7,000	12,000
Administrative expenses	96,000	
Distribution costs	100,000	
Land and buildings at cost	400,000	
Land and buildings – accumulated depreciation		80,000
Plant at cost	100,000	
Plant – accumulated depreciation		60,000
Office equipment at cost	20,000	
Office equipment – accumulated depreciation		10,000
Retained earnings		52,500
Debenture interest paid	2,000	
Ordinary dividend paid	1,600	
Bank	1,700	
Petty cash	200	
8% Debentures		50,000
	1,495,500	1,495,500

You are also provided with the following information:

i)   Inventory at 31 March 20X2 is valued at £52,000
ii)   Corporation tax for the year is estimated at £48,000
iii)   The outstanding debenture interest has not yet been accounted for.

You are required to prepare the income statement for the year ended 31 March 20X2 and the balance sheet at that date.

chapter 3:
PUBLISHED FINANCIAL STATEMENTS
OF LIMITED COMPANIES

1   What is the purpose of financial statements?

2   Briefly explain what is meant by financial statements showing a true and fair view or a fair presentation.

3   IAS 1 statements that financial statements must be prepared on the accruals basis. Which other important accounting principle must be followed?

4   Write out a pro-forma of the income statement.

5   List the items that should be disclosed under the heading of 'Current liabilities'.

6   List six of the items that should appear in a Directors' Report.

7   Fill in the gaps.

A .... is a component of an entity that has either been disposed of or is .... and represents a separate .... or .... of operation.

8   The draft income statement of Diverge Ltd for the year ended 31 December 20X3 is shown below.

	£'000
Revenue	12,134
Cost of sales	(5,451)
Gross profit	6,683
Distribution costs	(1,758)
Administrative expenses	(1,041)
Profit from operations	3,884
Interest payable	(305)
Profit before tax	3,579
Tax	(1,144)
Profit for the year	2,435

You have been given the following further information.

a)   The company closed one of its divisions during the year. The results of the discontinued operation are shown below.

	Discontinued operation £'000
Revenue	364
Cost of sales	236
Gross profit	128
Distribution costs	70
Administrative expenses	53
	5

b)   The loss on disposal of the discontinued operation was £142,000. This has been included in interest payable.

Redraft the income statement so that it complies with the requirements of IFRS 5 *Non-current assets held for sale and discontinued operations*. You need only give the minimum disclosure required.

9 Given below is the trial balance for Paparazzi Ltd as at 30 June 20X2.

	£'000	£'000
Land and buildings	2,100	
Plant and machinery	1,050	
Fixtures and fittings	380	
Motor vehicles	620	
Retained earnings		1,131
Ordinary share capital (50p ordinary shares)		2,500
Share premium		300
Trade receivables	2,500	
Trade payables		1,400
Inventory at 1 July 20X1	690	
Accruals		50
Prepayments	40	
Sales		15,200
Purchases	10,960	
Accumulated depreciation:		
Land and buildings		280
Plant and machinery		194
Fixtures and fittings		128
Motor vehicles		276
Bank	567	
7% loan stock		1,200
Provision for doubtful debts		92
Returns inwards	500	
Returns outwards		180
Interim dividend paid	120	
Debenture interest paid	84	
Distribution costs	1,200	
Administrative expenses	2,120	
	22,931	22,931

You are also given the following information.

i) The inventory at 30 June 20X2 was valued at £710,000

ii) Depreciation for the year has already been entered into the ledger accounts.

There have been no additions or disposals of property, plant and equipment during the year.

iii) The corporation tax charge for the year is estimated at £130,000

You are required to prepare the income statement for the year ended 30 June 20X2 and the balance sheet at that date.

10 You have been asked to assist in the preparation of the financial statements of Fun Ltd for the year ended 30 September 20X8. The company is a distributor of children's games. You have been provided with the extended trial balance of Fun Ltd as at 30 September 20X8, which is set out below.

You have been given the following further information.

a) The share capital of the business consists of ordinary shares with a nominal value of 25 pence.

b) The company has paid an interim dividend of 6 pence per share this year.

c) Depreciation has been calculated on all of the property, plant and equipment of the business and has already been entered into the distribution costs and administrative expenses ledger balances as shown on the extended trial balance.

d) The tax charge for the year has been calculated as £972,000.

e) Interest on the loan has been paid for the first eleven months of the year only, but no interest has been paid or charged for the final month of the year. The loan carries a rate of interest of 8% per annum of the balance outstanding on the loan.

Tasks

a) Make any additional adjustments you feel to be necessary to the balances in the extended trial balance as a result of the matters set out in the further information above. Set out your adjustments in the form of journal entries.

   Notes

   1 Narratives and dates are not required.
   2 Ignore any effect of these adjustments on the tax charge for the year as given above.

b) Taking account of any adjustments made in Part a), draft an income statement for the year ended 30 September 20X8 in accordance with International Accounting Standards/International Financial Reporting Standards.

   You are not required to produce notes to the accounts.

c) The directors are interested in expanding operations next year. They wish to be clear about the constituents of the equity on the balance sheet and on the impact that leasing equipment, rather than purchasing equipment, might have on the company's balance sheet. They would like you to attend the next meeting of the Board.

   Prepare notes to bring to the Board meeting dealing with the following matters.

   i)   How the balances on the share premium and the revaluation reserve arose.

   ii) The recommendation of one of the directors is to lease the assets as he says that this means that the asset can be kept off the balance sheet. Comment on this recommendation.

FUN LIMITED
EXTENDED TRIAL BALANCE AS AT 30 SEPTEMBER 20X8

	Trial balance		Adjustments		Income statement		Balance sheet	
	Debit £'000	Credit £'000	Debit £'000	Credit £'000	Debit £'000	Credit £'000	Debit £'000	Credit £'000
Trade receivables	2,863						2,863	
Bank overdraft		316						316
Interest	300				300			
Retained earnings		3,811						3,811
Provision for doubtful debts		114						114
Distribution costs	2,055		614		2,669			
Administrative expenses	1,684		358		2,042			
Returns inwards	232				232			
Sales		14,595				14,595		
Land – cost	2,293						2,293	
Buildings – cost	2,857						2,857	
Fixtures and fittings – cost	1,245						1,245	
Motor vehicles – cost	2,524						2,524	
Office equipment – cost	872						872	
Inventory	1,893		2,041	2,041	1,893	2,041	2,041	
Purchases	6,671				6,671			
Interim dividend	480				480			
Trade payables		804						804
Buildings – accumulated depreciation		261		51				312
Fixtures and fittings – accumulated depreciation		309		124				433
Motor vehicles – accumulated depreciation		573		603				1,176
Office equipment – accumulated depreciation		184		81				265
Prepayments	63						63	
Carriage inwards	87				87			
Returns outwards		146				146		
Accruals				113				113
Investments	2,244						2,244	
Loan		3,600						3,600
Ordinary share capital		2,000						2,000
Share premium		1,300						1,300
Revaluation reserve		350						350
Profit					2,408			2,408
TOTAL	28,363	28,363	3,013	3,013	16,782	16,782	17,002	17,002

11

11 You are employed by a firm of certified accountants and have been asked to prepare the financial statements of Franco Ltd (a company which distributes confectionery) for the year ending 31 March 20X5. A bookkeeper at the company has prepared an extended trial balance for the year ending 31 March 20X5; this includes the normal year-end adjustments. You have been asked to review the trial balance in the light of some further information which may be relevant to the accounts and to make any adjustments necessary before they are published.

The extended trial balance of Franco Ltd is set out below.

The following further information is provided.

a) The tax charge for the year has been agreed at £110,000.

b) Motor expenses of £10,000 and wages of £2,000 have been wrongly included in the general expenses figure in the trial balance. Of the remaining general expenses, £100,000 should be classified as administrative, the balance being distribution expenses.

c) Interest due on the long-term loan for the year needs to be provided for; it is charged at 10% per annum.

d) An audit fee of £9,000 needs to be provided for.

e) Included in the total salaries figure is £98,000 of directors' emoluments. £68,000 of directors' emoluments should be classed as administrative expenses, the remainder being distribution. £104,000 of salaries and wages (excluding directors' emoluments) should be classed as administrative expenses, the remainder being distribution expenses.

f) Rates and light and heat should be split equally between administration and distribution expenses.

g) £27,000 of motor expenses are to be classed as distribution, the remainder as administration expenses.

h) The depreciation charges should be classed as:

	Administration £	Distribution £
Buildings	3,000	1,000
Fixtures and fittings	4,000	1,000
Motor vehicles	2,000	8,000
Office equipment	1,000	–

i) The insurance payment should be split in the ratio of 75/25 between administration and distribution expenses respectively.

EXTENDED TRIAL BALANCE AS AT 31 MARCH 20X5

Folio	Description	Ledger balances DR £000	Ledger balances CR £000	Adjustments DR £000	Adjustments CR £000	Income statement DR £000	Income statement CR £000	Balance sheet balances DR £000	Balance sheet balances CR £000
	Revenue		2,470				2,470		
	Purchases	1,000				1,000			
	Salaries and wages	400				400			
	Motor expenses	27				27			
	Rates	25			5	20			
	Light and heat	32		4		36			
	Carriage inwards	14				14			
	Advertising	95				95			
	Inventories	215		225	225	215	225	225	
	Trade receivables	450						450	
	Provision for doubtful debts		6		3				9
	Increase in prov for doubtful debts			3		3			
	Cash in hand	1						1	
	Cash at bank	6						6	
	Trade payables		170						170
	Land (cost)	375						375	
	Buildings (cost)	200						200	
	Fixtures and fittings (cost)	35						35	
	Motor vehicles (cost)	94						94	
	Office equipment (cost)	20						20	
	Buildings (acc dep)		20		4				24
	Fixtures and fittings (acc dep)		18		5				23
	Motor vehicles (acc dep)		54		10				64
	Office equipment (acc dep)		4		1				5
	Depreciation - buildings			4		4			
	Depreciation - fixtures and fittings			5		5			
	Depreciation - motor vehicles			10		10			
	Depreciation - office equipment			1		1			
	Returns inwards	10				10			
	Dividend paid	30				30			
	Returns outwards		5				5		
	General expenses	135				135			
	Insurance	13			1	12			
	Retained earnings		160						160
	Prepayment			6				6	
	Accruals				4				4
	Share capital - ordinary shares		250						250
	Long-term loan		20						20
	Profit					683			683
		3,177	3,177	258	258	2,700	2,700	1,412	1,412

13

Tasks

a) Make any adjustments you feel necessary to the balances in the extended trial balance as a result of the matters set out in the further information above. Set out your adjustments in the form of journal entries. (Ignore the effect of any adjustments on the tax charge for the year).

b) Draft an income statement for the year ended 31 March 20X5 and a balance sheet as at that date in a form suitable for publication. (You are not required to prepare a statement of recognised income and expenses.)

c) You have been asked by the directors of the company to prepare a short report covering the following.

Inventories are valued at the lower of cost and net realisable value in the accounts in accordance with IAS 2. The directors would like you to explain how cost and net realisable value are derived.

Write a report which covers the required points.

12 You have been assigned to assist in the preparation of the financial statements of Dowango Ltd for the year ended 31 March 20X6. The company is a cash and carry operation that trades from a large warehouse on an industrial estate. You have been provided with the extended trial balance of Dowango Ltd on 31 March 20X6 which is set out below.

You have been given the following further information.

a) The share capital of the business consists of ordinary shares with a nominal value of £1.

b) The company has paid an interim dividend of 4p per share during the year.

c) Depreciation has been calculated on all of the property, plant and equipment of the business and has already been entered on a monthly basis into the distribution expenses and administration costs ledger balances as shown on the extended trial balance.

d) The tax charge for the year has been calculated as £211,000.

e) Interest on the long-term loan has been paid for six months of the year. No adjustment has been made for the interest due for the final six months of the year. Interest is charged on the loan at a rate of 10% per annum.

f) An advertising campaign was undertaken during the year at a cost of £19,000. No invoices have yet been received for this campaign and no adjustment for this expense has been made in the extended trial balance.

g) The investments consist of shares in a retail company that were purchased with a view to resale at a profit. Dowango Ltd own 2% of the share capital of the company. At the end of the year a valuation of the shares was obtained with a view to selling the shares in the forthcoming year. The shares were valued at £56,000.

DOWANGO LIMITED: EXTENDED TRIAL BALANCE
AS AT 31 MARCH 20X6

Description	Trial balance		Adjustments		Income statement		Balance sheet	
	Debit £'000	Credit £'000	Debit £'000	Credit £'000	Debit £'000	Credit £'000	Debit £'000	Credit £'000
Land (cost)	431						431	
Buildings (cost)	512						512	
Fixtures & fittings (cost)	389						389	
Motor vehicles (cost)	341						341	
Office equipment - (cost)	105						105	
Buildings - (accumulated depreciation)		184						184
Fixtures & fittings - (accumulated depreciation)		181						181
Motor vehicles - (accumulated depreciation)		204						204
Office equipment - (accumulated depreciation)		56						56
Inventories	298		365	365	298	365	365	
Investments	64						64	
Receivables	619						619	
Provision for doubtful debts		27						27
Prepayments			21				21	
Cash in hand	3						3	
Cash at bank		157						157
Payables		331						331
Accruals				41				41
Sales		5,391				5,391		
Purchases	2,988				2,988			
Returns inwards	39				39			
Returns outwards		31				31		
Carriage inwards	20				20			
Distribution expenses	1,092		23	11	1,104			
Administrative costs	701		18	10	709			
Interest charges	15				15			
Dividend paid	20				20			
Share capital		500						500
Retained earnings		275						275
Long-term loan		300						300
Profit					594			594
	7,637	7,637	427	427	5,787	5,787	2,850	2,850

Tasks

a) Make any adjustments you feel to be necessary to the balances in the extended trial balance as a result of the matters set out in the further information above. Set out your adjustments in the form of journal entries. Narratives are not required. (Ignore any effect of these adjustments on the tax charge for the year as given above.)

b) Draft an income statement for the year ended 31 March 20X6 and a balance sheet as at that date. (You are not required to prepare a statement of recognised income and expenses.)

13 You have been asked to assist in the preparation of the financial statements of Solu Ltd for the year ended 31 March 20X8. The company runs a wholesale stationery and confectionery business for retailers. You have been provided with the extended trial balance of Solu Ltd for the year ended 31 March 20X8 which is set out below.

You have also been given the following further information.

a) The share capital of the business consists of ordinary shares with a nominal value of 25p.

b) The company has paid an interim dividend of 2p per share.

c) The tax charge for the year has been calculated as £75,000.

d) Depreciation has been charged on all assets for the year and included in the trial balance figures for distribution costs and administrative expenses.

e) The interest on the long-term loan is charged at 10% per annum. It is paid twice a year in arrears. The charge for the first six months of the year is included in the trial balance.

f) The general provision for bad debts is to be adjusted to 2% of trade receivables.

SOLU LIMITED
EXTENDED TRIAL BALANCE 31 MARCH 20X8

Description	Trial balance Debit £'000	Trial balance Credit £'000	Adjustments Debit £'000	Adjustments Credit £'000	Income statement Debit £'000	Income statement Credit £'000	Balance sheet Debit £'000	Balance sheet Credit £'000
Land and buildings - cost	268						268	
Fixtures and fittings - cost	100						100	
Motor vehicles - cost	120						120	
Office equipment - cost	90						90	
Land and buildings - accumulated depreciation		50						50
Fixtures and fittings - accumulated depreciation		35						35
Motor vehicles - accumulated depreciation		65						65
Office equipment - accumulated depreciation		45						45
Investment	200						200	
Sales		4,090				4,090		
Purchases	1,800				1,800			
Inventories	300		320	320	300	320	320	
Receivables	500						500	
Provision for bad debts		1						1
Prepayments			15				15	
Bank overdraft		55						55
Payables		459						459
Accruals				40				40
Carriage inwards	25				25			
Distribution costs	1,050		10	5	1,055			
Administrative expenses	970		30	10	990			
Interest charges	10				10			
Dividend paid	32				32			
Share capital		400						400
Retained earnings		65						65
Long-term loan		200						200
Profit					198			198
Total	5,465	5,465	375	375	4,410	4,410	1,613	1,613

Tasks

a) Make the journal entries you feel to be necessary to the balances in the extended trial balance as a result of the matters set out in the further information above. Narratives are not required.

Notes

1 Ignore any effect of these adjustments on the tax charge for the year given above.

2 You must show any workings relevant to understanding your calculation of figures appearing in the financial statements.

b) Draft an income statement for the year ended 31 March 20X8 (after adjustments made in Task a).

(Note. You are not required to prepare a statement of recognised income and expenses.)

14 You work as an assistant accountant in an accountancy firm. Your manager has asked you to help with the preparation of the financial statements of Bathlea Ltd for the year ended 30 September 20X8. The company operates a warehouse which distributes computer components. The bookkeeper has provided you with the extended trial balance of Bathlea Ltd for the year ended 30 September 20X8, which is set out below.

The following further information has been supplied.

a) The share capital of the company consists of ordinary shares with a nominal value of £1.

b) The company has paid an interim dividend of 3p per share.

c) The tax charge for the year has been calculated as £11,000.

d) Depreciation has been charged on all assets for the year and included in the trial balance figures for distribution costs and administrative expenses.

e) The interest on the long-term loan is charged at 12% per annum and is paid monthly in arrears. The charge for the first eleven months of the year is included in the trial balance.

f) A debtor owing Bathlea Ltd £10,000 went into liquidation on 2 October 20X8. This has not been accounted for.

g) The general provision for bad debts is to be adjusted to 3% of trade receivables.

BATHLEA LIMITED: EXTENDED TRIAL BALANCE 30 SEPTEMBER 20X8

Description	Trial balance Debit £'000	Trial balance Credit £'000	Adjustments Debit £'000	Adjustments Credit £'000	Income statement Debit £'000	Income statement Credit £'000	Balance sheet Debit £'000	Balance sheet Credit £'000
Land and buildings - cost	300						300	
Fixtures and fittings - cost	220						220	
Motor vehicles - cost	70						70	
Office equipment - cost	80						80	
Land and buildings - accumulated depreciation		65						65
Fixtures and fittings - accumulated depreciation		43						43
Motor vehicles - accumulated depreciation		27						27
Office equipment - accumulated depreciation		35						35
Sales		3,509				3,509		
Purchases	1,600				1,600			
Inventories	200		250	250	200	250	250	
Receivables	370						370	
Provision for bad debts		5						5
Prepayments			10				10	
Bank overdraft		3						3
Payables		350						350
Accruals				9				9
Carriage inwards	91				91			
Distribution costs	860		7	10	857			
Administrative expenses	890		2		892			
Interest charges	11				11			
Interim dividend	15				15			
Share capital		500						500
Retained earnings		70						70
Long-term loan		100						100
Profit (loss)					93			93
Total	4,707	4,707	269	269	3,759	3,759	1,300	1,300

Tasks

a) Make the necessary journal entries as a result of the further information given above. Dates and narratives are not required.

Notes

1 Ignore any effect of these adjustments on the tax charge for the year given above.
2 You must show any workings relevant to these adjustments.

b) Draft an income statement for the year ended 30 September 20X8 and a balance sheet as at that date (after adjustments made in Task a)).

c) There is a law suit pending against Bathlea Ltd. There is a remote possibility that it will result in Bathlea Ltd having to pay a customer compensation of £10,000 plus court costs. No account has been taken of this in the extended trial balance. The directors wish to know if it should be accrued.

chapter 4:
REPORTING FINANCIAL PERFORMANCE

1   At 1 April 20X1 a company had in issue 1 million 50 pence ordinary shares. On 1 August a further 400,000 50 pence ordinary shares were issued.

An extract from the income statement for the year ending 31 March 20X2 is given below.

	£'000
Profit before tax	240
Tax	70
Profit for the year	170
Dividends paid:	
Ordinary dividend	50

What is the earnings per share for the year?

2   Explain the difference between an accounting policy and an accounting estimate. Give an example of both an accounting policy and an accounting estimate.

3   A company can only change an accounting policy if the change is required by a standard. True or false?

4   A company which started in business on 1 January 20X0 has never depreciated its land and buildings. However for the year ended 31 December 20X2 it has been decided by the directors that depreciation should be charged on the buildings element based on the assumption that the buildings have a useful economic life of 50 years.

The buildings were purchased on 1 January 20X0 for a cost of £600,000 and they have remained in the accounts at that figure. The profit for each of the first three years of trading is as shown below.

Year ending:
31 December 20X0   £60,000
31 December 20X1   £80,000
31 December 20X2   £90,000 (after charging depreciation on the buildings)

Complete the figures required in the movement of reserves shown below.

	20X2 £	20X1 £
Retained earnings at the beginning of the year:		
As previously reported		
Change in accounting policy		
Restated	————	————
Retained earnings for the year		
Retained earnings at the end of the year	————	————

5   During the year ended 30 April 20X2 a company made a profit before tax of £150,000. The estimated corporation tax charge for the year was £40,000. On 1 May 20X1 there were already 500,000 £1 ordinary shares in issue. On that date the company issued a further 200,000 ordinary shares at a price of £1.40 per share.

During the year the company revalued some of its non-current assets upwards by £70,000. An ordinary dividend of 5 pence per share was paid.

The shareholders' funds at 1 May 20X1 (before accounting for the share issue) were made up as follows:

	£
£1 ordinary shares	500,000
Share premium	100,000
Revaluation reserve	30,000
Retained earnings	180,000
	810,000

You are required to prepare the following for the year ended 30 April 20X2 in as much detail as is possible from the question:

i)   The income statement
ii)   The statement of recognised income and expense
iii) Total movements in equity

6   What are the main requirements of IFRS 8 *Operating segments*?

7   After the financial statements for the year ended 31 December 20X3 have been published, it is discovered that one of the accounts staff had stolen money from the company throughout 20X3. He has done this by submitting false invoices from fictitious suppliers. As a result, the purchases figure in the 20X3 financial statements is overstated and the amount included is material.

What action should be taken, if any, regarding the financial statements?

chapter 5:
THE CASH FLOW STATEMENT

1   Explain why profit is not always the same as cash flow.

2   An extract from a company's income statement for the year ended 31 December 20X1 is given:

	£
Sales	560,000
Cost of sales	300,000
Gross profit	260,000
Other expenses	160,000
Profit from operations	100,000

Other expenses include £20,000 of depreciation, £10,000 of interest payable and £90,000 of wages costs. The tax expense for the year was £25,000.

Extracts from the balance sheet are also given below:

	20X1	20X0
	£	£
Inventory	30,000	25,000
Receivables	40,000	42,000
Payables	28,000	32,000

You are required to calculate the net cash from operating activities using the indirect method.

3   Given below is an extract from a company's balance sheet:

	Year ended 31 March	
	20X2	20X1
	£'000	£'000
Trade payables	340	380
Corporation tax	100	94
Accrued interest	8	13

The income statement shows that interest payable for the year was £32,400 and the corporation tax charge was £98,000.

What figures would appear in the cash flow statement for:

i)   interest paid?
ii) tax paid?

4   An extract from a company's balance sheet is given below:

	Year ended 30 June	
	20X2	20X1
	£'000	£'000
Property, plant and equipment at cost	1,340	1,250
Less: accumulated depreciation	(560)	(480)
	780	770

During the year items with a cost of £140,000 and net book value of £98,000 were sold at a loss of £23,000.

You are required to calculate:

i)   cash paid to acquire property, plant and equipment during the year
ii) proceeds of the sale of property, plant and equipment in the year
iii) the depreciation charge for the year

5   The net book value of a company's property, plant and equipment at 1 April 20X1 was £830,000 and at 31 March 20X2 £890,000. The depreciation charge for the year had been £120,000 and items with a cost of £60,000 were sold for £35,000 giving a profit of £6,000.

What is the figure for cash paid to acquire new property, plant and equipment which will appear in the cash flow statement?

6   Given below is the balance sheet of Bodice Ltd at 30 April 20X2 together with comparative figures and the income statement for the year ended on that date.

Balance sheet as at 30 April 20X2

	30 April 20X2 £'000	30 April 20X1 £'000
Non-current assets:		
Property, plant and equipment at cost	612	408
Less: depreciation	(204)	(128)
	408	280
Current assets:		
Inventories	110	94
Trade receivables	85	77
Investments	68	17
Cash and cash equivalents	–	24
	263	212
Total assets	671	492
Current liabilities:		
Trade payables	68	43
Tax liabilities	42	34
Bank overdraft	17	–
	127	77
Net current assets	136	135
Non-current liabilities:		
Long-term loans	180	130
Total liabilities	307	207
Net assets	364	285
Equity:		
Share capital	60	50
Share premium	25	20
Retained earnings	279	215
Total equity	364	285

Income statement for the year ended 30 April 20X2

	£'000
Profit from operations	165
Investment income	8
Loss on sale of property, plant and equipment	(9)
Finance costs	(17)
Profit before tax	147
Tax	(38)
Profit for the year attributable to equity holders	109

During the year items of property, plant and equipment were sold which had originally cost £43,000 and had a net book value of £26,000.

The current asset investments are to be regarded as cash equivalents.

Prepare the cash flow statement and related notes, in accordance with IAS 7, for the year ended 30 April 20X2.

7   Given below are extracts from the balance sheet of a company.

	Year ended 30 June	
	20X2	20X1
	£'000	£'000
Current asset investments	14,000	8,000
Cash at bank and in hand	1,000	3,000
Bank overdraft	12,000	–
Long-term loans	30,000	20,000

The current asset investments qualify as cash equivalents.

You are required to calculate the movement in cash and cash equivalents for the year ended 30 June 20X2.

8   What are the advantages and limitations of published cash flow statements?

9   Given below is the summarised cash flow statement for Chadd Ltd for the year ended 31 May 20X2.

Cash flow from operating activities

	£'000
Profit from operations	399
Depreciation	366
Increase in inventories	(159)
Increase in receivables	(190)
Increase in trade payables	94
Cash generated from operations	510
Interest paid	(75)
Corporation tax paid	(64)
Net cash from operating activities	371
Cash flow from investing activities	
Purchase of property, plant and equipment	(670)
Cash flow from financing activities	
Proceeds from long-term loan	180
Dividends paid	(70)
Decrease in cash for the year	(189)

Explain what this cash flow statement indicates about the strategies and performance of the management of the company during the year.

10 You have been asked to assist in the preparation of financial statements for Paton Ltd for the year ended 30 September 20X1. The income statement and balance sheets of Paton Ltd are set out below.

PATON LIMITED
INCOME STATEMENT FOR THE YEAR 30 SEPTEMBER 20X1

	£'000
Revenue	24,732
Cost of sales	11,129
Gross profit	13,603
Profit on the sale of non-current assets	131
Distribution costs	4,921
Administration expenses	2,875
Profit before interest	5,938
Finance costs	392
Profit before taxation	5,546
Tax	1,821
Profit for the financial year	3,725

PATON LIMITED
BALANCE SHEET AS AT 30 SEPTEMBER 20X1

	20X1 £'000	20X0 £'000
Non-current assets	13,383	9,923
Investment in MacNeal Ltd	5,000	-
	18,383	9,923
Current assets		
Inventories	7,420	6,823
Trade receivables	4,122	3,902
Cash	102	1,037
	11,644	11,762
Total assets	30,027	21,685
Current liabilities		
Trade payables	1,855	1,432
Taxation	1,821	1,327
	3,676	2,759
Net current assets	7,968	9,003
Long-term loan	5,000	1,500
	8,676	4,259
Net assets	21,351	17,426
Equity		
Share capital	10,000	9,000
Share premium	3,500	3,000
Retained earnings	7,851	5,426
	21,351	17,426

You have been given the following further information.

- A non-current asset costing £895,000 with accumulated depreciation of £372,000 was sold in the year. The total depreciation charge for the year was £2,007,000.

- All sales and purchases were on credit. Other expenses were paid for in cash.

Task

Provide a reconciliation of profit from operations to net cash from operating activities for Paton Ltd for the year ended 30 September 20X1.

11 You are presented with the following information for Evans.

EVANS
INCOME STATEMENT FOR THE YEAR ENDED 31 OCTOBER 20X1

	£'000
Revenue	2,000
Cost of goods sold	(1,350)
Gross profit	650
Distribution costs	(99)
Administrative expenses	(120)
Profit from operations	431
Gain on disposal of non-current assets	10
Dividend received	12
Finance costs	(35)
Profit before taxation	418
Tax	(125)
Profit	293

EVANS
BALANCE SHEETS AS AT 31 OCTOBER

	20X0		20X1	
	£'000	£'000	£'000	£'000
Non-current assets				
Furniture at cost *200 addih'n*	700		900	
Less depreciation	200		270	
		500		630
Vehicles at cost	820		890	
Less depreciation	310		340	
		510		550
Investments, at cost		80		155
		1,090		1,335
Current assets				
Inventory	505		486	
Receivables	577		790	
Cash and bank	10		2	
		1,092		1,278
		2,182		2,613
Total assets				
Current liabilities				
Payables	546		560	
Taxation	106		125	
		(652)		(685)
Non-current liabilities				
12% Loan notes		(150)		(50)
Total liabilities		(802)		(735)
Net assets		1,380		1,878
Equity				
Ordinary share				
capital	1,000		1,200	
Share premium	270		315	
Retained earnings	110		363	
		1,380		1,878

Additional information for the year ended 31 October 20X1

a) Vehicles which had cost £155,000 were sold during the year when their net book value was £65,000.

b) There were no prepaid or accrued expenses at the beginning or end of the year.

c) Dividends of £40,000 were paid during the year.

Tasks

i) Prepare a cash flow statement for Evans for the year ended 31 October 20X1. State the accounting standard you have applied, and show any additional notes and reconciliations required.

ii) Briefly explain why cash flow statements are useful to external users.

12 You are presented with the following information for Dawson.

DAWSON LIMITED
BALANCE SHEET AS AT

	31 May 20X0		31 May 20X1	
	£'000	£'000	£'000	£'000
Non-current assets				
Intangible		460		450
Tangible		1,200		1,400
Investments		180		240
		1,840		2,090
Current assets				
Inventory	450		500	
Receivables	270		300	
Bank	-		50	
		720		850
Total assets		2,560		2,940
Current liabilities				
Trade payables	200		220	
Bank overdraft	50		-	
Taxation	120		125	
		370		345
Non-current liabilities				
Long-term loans		40		150
Total liabilities		410		495
Net assets		2,150		2,445
Equity and liabilities				
Equity				
Ordinary share capital		1,000		1,200
Share premium		-		15
Retained earnings		1,150		1,230
		2,150		2,445

DAWSON LIMITED
INCOME STATEMENT FOR THE YEAR ENDED 31 MAY 20X1

	£'000
Profit before tax	310
Tax	120
Profit for the year	190

Additional information for the year ended 31 May 20X1

a)   Non-current assets with a net book value of £160,000 were sold for a profit of £85,000.

b)   Depreciation charged on tangible non-current assets was £305,000.

c)   Interest charged in the income statement was £24,000.

Retained earnings at 1 June 20X0	1,150
Profit for the year	190
Dividend paid	(110)
	1,230

d)   There were no prepaid or accrued expenses at the beginning or end of the year.

Tasks

i)   Prepare a cash flow statement for Dawson for the year ended 31 May 20X1 in accordance with recognised accounting standards.

ii)   Review the cash flow statement you have prepared in part i) and comment on the financial position of Dawson.

chapter 6:
NON-CURRENT ASSETS

1   In each of the following situations determine how much should be capitalised in the balance sheet as the cost of property, plant and equipment assets. Explain your treatment of each item of cost.

   i)   A car was purchased for a total invoiced amount of £14,500. This was after deducting the part exchange value of an old car of £3,000 and included road tax of £150.

   ii)   A building was purchased for £100,000. During the purchase legal fees of £4,000 were incurred and before the building was used it was completely redecorated at a cost of £12,000.

   iii) A machine was purchased at a cost of £24,000. Delivery costs totalled £1,000 and the cost of installing the machine was £2,000. As the machine was a significant technological advance on the old machines used the employees using the machine had to attend a training course at a cost of £3,500.

   iv)   Repairs to a machine totalled £6,000 for a year and during the year the machine engine was replaced by a more powerful engine that will increase production speed at a cost of £15,000.

2   i)   What are the requirements of IAS 16 *Property, plant and equipment*, if items are to be revalued?

   ii)   A property was purchased on 1 April 20X0 for £160,000. Depreciation policy is to depreciate properties over a period of 40 years. On 31 March 20X2 the property is to be revalued to £200,000.

         What is the double entry required to record the revaluation?

   iii) What would be the depreciation charge for the year ending 31 March 20X3?

3   i)   What is the purpose of depreciation? In your answer refer to any accounting concepts that are relevant.

   ii)   A machine was purchased on 1 July 20X0 for £30,000 and was depreciated on the reducing balance method at the rate of 40%. On 1 July 20X2 the directors of the company decided to change the depreciation method to the straight line method. It was felt at that date that the machine had a remaining useful life of three years and an estimated residual value of £1,800. What is the depreciation charge for the year ended 30 June 20X3?

iii) A machine was purchased on 1 January 20X0 for £80,000 and was to be depreciated over a period of 10 years using the straight line method. On 1 January 20X2 it was decided that the machine had a total useful life of just 7 years. What is the depreciation charge for the year ending 31 December 20X2?

4   On 1 January 20X0 a building was purchased for £240,000 and was to be depreciated over its useful life of 50 years. On 1 January 20X4 it was revalued to £460,000 with no change in estimated useful life. On 31 December 20X5 the building was sold for £500,000.

What is the profit on disposal?

5   An extract from a company's trial balance at its year end is given below:

	£'000	£'000
Land and buildings at cost	950	
Plant and machinery at cost	480	
Fixtures and fittings at cost	200	
Land and buildings – accumulated depreciation		285
Plant and machinery – accumulated depreciation		250
Fixtures and fittings – accumulated depreciation		75

You are also given the following information about transactions in the year.

i) An additional building was purchased for £100,000. The depreciation charge for the year for the buildings was £19,000.

ii) Plant and machinery with a cost of £45,000 and a net book value of £28,000 was sold during the year. The depreciation charge for the year was £94,000.

iii) Fixtures and fittings costing £34,000 were purchased in the year. There were also sales of old fixtures and fittings which had originally cost £10,000 but were already fully written off. The depreciation charge for the year was £15,000.

You are required to draft the property, plant and equipment disclosure note required by IAS 16.

6   i)   What is the definition of an investment property from IAS 40?

     ii)   Briefly summarise how IAS 40 requires investment properties to be treated in financial statements and the reasons for this treatment.

7   i)   Define research and development.

     ii)   What criteria must be met according to IAS 38 if development expenditure is to be capitalised in the balance sheet?

     iii) If development expenditure is capitalised in the balance sheet what is its subsequent treatment in the financial statements?

8 i) What is the difference between goodwill and other intangible non-current assets?
ii) How should internally generated goodwill be treated in the financial statements?

9 Briefly explain the requirements of IAS 36 *Impairment of assets*.

10 The directors of a company have asked you a number of questions. Prepare notes to answer them referring to accounting standards where appropriate.

i) An independent valuer has valued the land and buildings at £550,000. Currently they are in the trial balance at cost £268,000, and accumulated depreciation of £50,000. The directors have asked you if it is possible to show this valuation rather than the cost of the assets in the trial balance and, if so, to detail the entries needed to show the increased value of the non-current assets in the accounts.

ii) The directors understand that the accounts are prepared under the accruals concept. They are unsure what this means and have asked you to explain it briefly using an example.

1 What are the IAS 2 definitions of:

i) Cost of inventory?
ii) Net realisable value?

2 A business sells three products and at the balance sheet date details of the inventories of these products are:

	Cost	Selling price	Selling costs
	£	£	£
Basic	14,300	20,700	2,400
Standard	21,600	24,000	3,000
Premium	17,500	28,600	1,800

At what value should the closing inventories appear in the balance sheet?

3 A business has inventories of its single product of 2,000 units on 1 April 20X2 valued at £6.40 per unit. During April the following movements of inventory took place.

5 April	Purchases	1,000 units @ £7.00
12 April	Sales	2,500 units @ £12.00
17 April	Purchases	2,000 units @ £7.40
26 April	Purchases	1,500 units @ £7.80
30 April	Sales	3,000 units @ £12.00

Calculate the closing inventory value at 30 April 2002 and the gross profit earned for the month using each of the following costing methods:

i) FIFO
ii) AVCO

4   A company estimates that its corporation tax liability for the year ended 30 June 20X1 is £113,000. During the year to 30 June 20X2 the amount actually paid to Her Majesty's Revenue and Customs (HMRC) was £108,000. The estimate for the corporation tax liability for the year ended 30 June 20X2 is £129,000.

i)   What is the corporation tax charge in the income statement for the year ending 30 June 20X2?

ii)   What is the corporation tax liability to appear in the balance sheet at 30 June 20X2?

5   In the context of corporation tax explain what are meant by permanent differences and temporary differences. Give one example of each.

6   At 30 April 20X2 a company has the following balances on its trial balance.

	Dr £'000	Cr £'000
Corporation tax	16	
Deferred tax		150

The estimated corporation tax charge for the year to 30 April 20X2 is £217,000 and the deferred tax liability is to be increased to £180,000.

Show how this information would be reflected in the income statement for the year ended 30 April 20X2 and the balance sheet at that date.

7   Explain the appropriate accounting treatment in each of the following situations.

i)   A manufacturer has always had a policy of replacing defective goods that have been returned by customers. At the balance sheet date it is estimated that goods already sold that will be returned after the year end as defective have a cost of £4,000.

ii)   A business has valued one line of its inventory at cost of £53,000 at the balance sheet date of 31 May 20X2. During the month of June all of this inventory is sold for £42,000.

iii) A company has a year end of 31 March 20X2. During March 20X2 a board decision was made to close a division at an estimated cost of £100,000. On 5 April 20X2 this was announced to the workforce and notification was sent to major suppliers and customers.

iv)   A company is being sued by an employee for injury at work. The employee is seeking damages of £250,000 and the company lawyers think that it is possible although unlikely that the employee will win the case.

v)   A company has a year end of 30 April 20X2. On 14 May 20X2 it issues 400,000 additional £1 ordinary shares (current issued share capital 500,000 shares) at a price of £1.60 per share.

8   The Directors of Franco Ltd have drawn your attention to three matters and requested your advice on how these should be treated.

   i)   An issue of shares was made on 10 April 20X5. Fifty thousand 50p ordinary shares were issued at a premium of 25p.

   ii)   A customer owing £30,000 to Franco Ltd on 31 March 20X5 went into liquidation on 3 April 20X5. The £30,000 is still unpaid and it is unclear whether any monies will be received.

   iii) The company is awaiting the outcome of a legal suit; an independent lawyer has assessed that it is probable that the company will gain £25,000 from it.

   Write a memo to the directors of Franco Ltd outlining the required treatment for each of the three events.

chapter 8:
FURTHER ACCOUNTING STANDARDS

1 What is the general rule regarding recognition of assets and liabilities from the IASB's Framework?

2 Birtles Ltd owns a property with a book value of £850,000. On 1 April 20X1 Birtles Ltd sells the property to National Bank for £1,000,000 with an agreement that Birtles Ltd will repurchase the property in two years time for £1,200,000. Birtles Ltd still occupies the property.

For the year ended 31 March 20X2 this transaction has been treated as the sale of the property and a profit of £150,000 has been recognised in the income statement. The property no longer appears in the balance sheet.

State whether or not you believe that the accounting treatment is appropriate to reflect the substance of the transaction. If not, discuss how the transaction should be accounted for, giving reasons for your treatment.

3 i)   Define a finance lease.
    ii)   Define an operating lease.
    iii) Explain the accounting treatment of finance leases in the accounts of the lessee.
    iv)   Explain the accounting treatment of operating leases in the accounts of the lessee.
    v)   Why are finance leases and operating leases accounted for differently?

4 What conditions should be met before revenue from the sale of goods is recognised in the financial statements?

chapter 9:
INTERPRETING FINANCIAL STATEMENTS

1   A business has revenue for a year of £425,000, cost of sales of £280,000 and other operating expenses of £98,000.

What is the gross profit margin and the net profit margin?

2   Given below is a summarised income statement and balance sheet for a company.

Income statement for the year ended 30 April 20X2

	£'000
Revenue	989
Cost of sales	(467)
Gross profit	522
Other operating expenses	(308)
	214
Interest payable	(34)
Profit before tax	180
Corporation tax	(48)
	132

Balance sheet as at 30 April 20X2

	£'000
Non-current assets	1,200
Net current assets	200
	1,400
Long-term loan	(400)
	1,000
Share capital and reserves	1,000

Calculate the following ratios for the year.

i)   Gross profit margin
ii)   Net profit margin
iii) Return on capital employed
iv)   Asset turnover
v)   Return on equity
vi)   Interest cover
vii) Gearing

3   Given below are extracts from a company's income statement and balance sheet.

Income statement for the year ended 30 June 20X2 – extract

	£	£
Revenue		772,400
Less: cost of sales		
Opening inventory	53,700	
Purchases	512,300	
	566,000	
Less: closing inventory	58,600	
		507,400
Gross profit		265,000

Balance sheet at 30 June 20X2 – extract

	£
Receivables	98,400
Payables	86,200
Bank overdraft	6,300

Calculate the following ratios.

i)   Current ratio
ii)   Quick (acid test) ratio
iii) Receivables days
iv)   Inventory turnover
v)   Inventory days
vi)   Payables days

4   i)   Explain why a highly geared company may appear to be more risky that one with a lower level of gearing.

ii)   State two formulae that can be used to measure how highly geared a company is.

5   What are the limitations of using ratio analysis to assess financial performance?

6   Given below are a range of financial ratios for two companies that both operate in the retail trade.

	Rigby Ltd	Rialto Ltd
Gross profit margin	60%	32%
Net profit margin	28%	10%
Asset turnover	0.80 times	2.2 times
ROCE	22%	22%
Current ratio	2.0	1.8
Quick ratio	1.2	0.4
Inventory turnover	4.8 times	10.3 times
Receivables days	41 days	3 days
Payables days	62 days	70 days
Gearing	33%	50%
Interest cover	16 times	5 times

i)   Comment upon what the ratios indicate about each business.

ii)   One of the businesses is a supermarket and the other is a jeweller who supplies some goods on credit to long standing customers. Identify which business is which.

7   Given below are the income statements and balance sheet for Garth Ltd for the last two years.

Income statement	Year ended	
	31 March 20X2	31 March 20X1
	£'000	£'000
Revenue	470	390
Cost of sales	287	224
Gross profit	183	166
Operating expenses	97	73
Finance costs	25	14
Profit before tax	61	79
Tax	15	20
Profit after tax	46	59

Balance sheet

	31 March 20X2 £'000	31 March 20X1 £'000
Property, plant and equipment	760	566
Current assets		
Inventory	36	37
Receivables	110	62
Bank and cash	16	20
	162	119
Total assets	922	685
Current liabilities		
Trade payables	41	25
Corporation tax	15	20
Other payables	16	20
	72	65
Non-current liabilities		
Long-term loan	350	150
Total liabilities	422	215
Net assets	500	470
Share capital: £1 ordinary shares	300	300
Share premium	50	50
Retained earnings	150	120
	500	470

Write a report to a shareholder in the company identifying the main changes in the management of the company in the last two years.

8   The directors of Dowango Ltd have asked to have a meeting with you. They are intending to ask the bank for a further long-term loan to enable them to purchase a company which has retail outlets. The directors have identified two possible companies to take over and they intend to purchase the whole of the share capital of one of the two targeted companies. The directors have obtained the latest financial statements of the two companies in summary form, and have also sent you a letter with some questions that they would like you to answer. The financial statements and the letter are set out below.

SUMMARY INCOME STATEMENTS

	Company A £'000	Company B £'000
Revenue	800	2,100
Cost of sales	440	1,050
Gross profit	360	1,050
Expenses	160	630
Net profit before interest and tax	200	420

SUMMARY BALANCE SHEETS

	Company A £'000	Company B £'000
Non-current assets	620	1,640
Net current assets	380	1,160
Long-term loan	(400)	(1,100)
	600	1,700
Equity (share capital and retained earnings)	600	1,700

DOWANGO LTD

Dear AAT student

In preparation for discussions about a possible loan to Dowango Ltd, the bank has asked to see the latest financial statements of Dowango Ltd. We wish to ensure that the financial statements show the company in the best light. In particular, we wish to ensure that the assets of the business are shown at their proper value. We would like to discuss with you the following issues.

a) The non-current assets of our company are undervalued. We have received a professional valuation of the land and buildings which shows that they are worth more than is stated in our financial statements. The land has a current market value of £641,000 and the buildings are valued at £558,000. The land and buildings currently have net book values of £431,000 and £328,000 respectively.

b) The investments are recorded in our trial balance at cost. We realise that the market value of the investments is less than the cost, but since we have not yet sold them, we have not made a loss on it and so we should continue to show them at cost.

c) Inventories are recorded in our balance sheet at cost. Most of our inventory is worth more than this as we could sell it for more than we paid for it. Only a few items would sell for less than we paid for them. We have worked out the real value of our inventory as follows.

	Cost £'000	Sales prices £'000
Undervalued items	340	460
Overvalued items	25	15
Total	365	475

We have set out a number of questions we would like answered at our meeting in an appendix to this letter. We would also like you to advise us at that meeting on the profitability and return on capital of the two companies targeted for takeover (whose financial statements we have already sent to you) and on the reporting implications if we purchase one of the companies.

Yours sincerely

The directors

Task

i) The questions from the appendix to the directors' letter are shown below. Write a memo to the directors answering these questions, which relate to the financial statements of Dowango Ltd. Explain your answers, where relevant, by reference to company law, accounting concepts and applicable accounting standards.

    1)   Can we show the land and buildings at valuation rather than cost?

    2)   If we did so, how would the valuation of land and buildings be reflected in the financial statements?

    3)   Would revaluing the land and buildings have any effect upon the gearing ratio of the company and would this assist us in our attempt to get a loan from the bank?

    4)   What effect would a revaluation have upon the future results of the company?

  ii)   Can we continue to show the investments at cost?

  iii)   What is the best value for inventory that we can show in our balance sheet in the light of the information we have given you about sales price?

Advise the directors as to which of the two companies targeted for takeover is the more profitable and which one provides the higher return on capital. Your answer should include calculation of the following ratios.

  i)   Return on capital employed

  ii)   Net profit margin

  iii)   Asset turnover

You should also calculate and comment on at least one further ratio of your choice, for which you have sufficient information, which would be relevant to determining which of the companies is more profitable or provides the greater return on capital.

9   You have been asked by the directors of Binns Ltd, a distributor of domestic and industrial refuse containers, to analyse the financial statements of a potential supplier. They have identified a company called Gone Ltd as a potential supplier of containers. They have obtained the latest financial statements of the company, in summary form, which are set out below.

GONE LIMITED
SUMMARY INCOME STATEMENT
FOR THE YEAR ENDED 31 DECEMBER

	20X7	20X6
	£'000	£'000
Revenue	1,800	1,300
Cost of sales	1,098	715
Gross profit	702	585
Expenses	504	315
Net profit before interest and tax	198	270

GONE LIMITED
SUMMARY BALANCE SHEETS
AS AT 31 DECEMBER

	20X7		20X6	
	£'000	£'000	£'000	£'000
Non-current assets		3,463		1,991
Current assets	460		853	
Current liabilities	(383)		(406)	
Net current assets		77		447
Long-term loan		(1,506)		(500)
Net assets		2,034		1,938
Share capital		800		800
Revaluation reserve		164		164
Retained earnings		1,070		974
		2,034		1,938

The industry average ratios are as follows.

	20X7	20X6
Return on capital employed	13.4%	13.0%
Gross profit percentage	44.5%	43.2%
Net profit percentage	23.6%	23.2%
Current ratio	2.0:1	1.9:1
Gearing	36%	34%

Task

Prepare a report for the directors recommending whether or not to use Gone Ltd as a supplier for Binns Ltd given the information contained in the financial statements and the industry averages supplied. Your answer should comment on the profitability, liquidity and the level of gearing in the company, and how they have changed over the two years, and compare it with the industry as a whole. The report should include calculation of the following ratios for the two years.

a) Return on capital employed
b) Gross profit percentage
c) Net profit percentage
d) Current ratio
e) Gearing

10 Animalets plc is a large company with a number of subsidiaries. The group manufactures and distributes pet food and pet accessories. It is considering buying some shares in Superpet Ltd, a small company which makes toys and novelties for pets.

You have been given the financial statements for Superpet Ltd for the year ended 30 September 20X8.

SUPERPET LIMITED
INCOME STATEMENT FOR THE YEAR ENDED 30 SEPTEMBER

	20X8		20X7	
	£'000	£'000	£'000	£'000
Revenue,				
continuing operations		2,000		1,500
Cost of sales:				
opening inventories	300		200	
purchases	900		800	
closing inventories	(350)		(300)	
		850		700
Gross profit		1,150		800
Depreciation		65		50
Other expenses		132		118
Profit on sale of				
non-current asset		5		-
Profit from operations		958		632
Finance cost (interest paid)		10		7
Profit before tax		948		625
Tax		300		200
Profit for the year		648		425

SUPERPET LIMITED
BALANCE SHEET AS AT 30 SEPTEMBER

	20X8		20X7	
	£'000	£'000	£'000	£'000
Non-current assets		1,138		638
Current assets				
Inventories	350		300	
Receivables	400		250	
Cash	120		60	
	870		610	
Current liabilities				
Trade payables	370		248	
Taxation	300		200	
	670		448	
Net current assets		200		162
		1,338		800
Long-term liabilities				
Long-term loan		(100)		(70)
		1,238		730
Equity				
Share capital		220		200
Share premium account		50		30
Revaluation reserve		50		50
Retained earnings		918		450
		1,238		730

Tasks

a) Prepare a report to the directors of Animalets plc which considers Superpet's position and performance. Your report should be based on the following ratios only.

   i)   Gross profit ratio
   ii) Current ratio
   iii) Acid test (quick) ratio
   iv) Gearing ratio

   You are not expected to include recommendations in your report.

b) The directors of Animalets want to know how much cash Superpet received from operating activities for the year ended 30 September 20X8. Prepare a reconciliation of profit from operations to cash flow from operating activities for this period.

11 Georgina Grieg is deciding whether to lend some money to Gint Ltd. She has asked you to comment on the financial position of the company and to explain certain aspects of the financial statements of the company. She has given you the financial statements of Gint Ltd.

GINT LIMITED
INCOME STATEMENTS
FOR THE YEAR ENDED 31 MARCH

	20X3	20X2
	£'000	£'000
Revenue	3,851	3,413
Cost of sales	2,002	1,775
Gross profit	1,849	1,638
Distribution costs	782	737
Administrative expenses	515	491
Profit from operations	552	410
Finance costs	46	41
Profit before tax	506	369
Tax	126	92
Profit for the year	380	277

GINT LIMITED
BALANCE SHEETS AS AT 31 MARCH

	20X3	20X2
	£'000	£'000
Non-current assets:		
Property, plant and equipment	4,372	4,341
Current assets:		
Inventories	1,157	716
Trade receivables	446	509
Prepayments	23	19
Cash and cash equivalents	37	57
	1,663	1,301
Total assets	6,035	5,642
Current liabilities:		
Trade payables	406	392
Accruals	31	26
Tax liabilities	126	92
	563	510
Net current assets	1,100	791
Non-current liabilities:		
Long-term loans	600	500
Total liabilities	1,163	1,010
Net assets	4,872	4,632
Equity:		
Share capital	1,000	1,000
Retained earnings	3,872	3,632
	4,872	4,632

Task 1

Write a letter to Georgina Grieg that includes the following.

a)   A calculation of the following ratios of Gint Ltd for each of the two years.

    i)   Current ratio
    ii)   Quick ratio/acid test
    iii)   Gearing ratio
    iv)   Interest cover

b)   An explanation of the meaning of each ratio

c)   Comments on the financial position of Gint Ltd as shown by the ratios

d)   A statement on how the financial position has changed over the two years covered by the financial statements

e)   A conclusion on whether Georgina Grieg should lend money to Gint Ltd. Base your conclusion only on the ratios calculated and analysis performed

Task 2

Answer the following questions asked by Georgina Grieg.

a)   What is the monetary value of the equity, the assets and liabilities in Gint Ltd?
b)   How are these related in money terms in the accounting equation as at 31 March 20X3?

12   Michael Beacham has been asked to lend money to Goodall Ltd for a period of three years. He employed a financial adviser to advise him whether to make a loan to the company. The financial adviser has obtained the financial statements of the company for the past two years, calculated some ratios and found the industry averages. However, she was unable to complete her report. Michael has asked you to analyse the ratios and to advise him on whether he should make a loan to Goodall Ltd. The ratios are set out below.

	20X3	20X2	Industry average
Gearing ratio	67%	58%	41%
Interest cover	1.2	2.3	4.6
Quick ratio/acid test	0.5	0.8	1.1
Return on equity	9%	13%	19%

Write a report for Michael Beacham that includes the following.

a)   An explanation of the meaning of each ratio.

b)   A comment on Goodall's financial position and the performance of the company as shown by the ratios.

c)   A statement of how the financial position and performance have changed over the two years, and how they compare with the industry average.

d)   A conclusion on whether Michael should lend money to Goodall Ltd. Base your conclusion only on the ratios calculated and the analysis performed.

chapter 10:
THE CONSOLIDATED BALANCE SHEET

1   IAS 27 *Consolidated and separate financial statements*, identifies five situations where one entity is the parent of another entity. What are these five situations?

2   On 1 April 20X0 P Ltd acquired 100% of the ordinary issued share capital of S Ltd when S Ltd's reserves were £45,000. At 31 March 20X2 the balance sheets of both companies were as follows.

	P Ltd	S Ltd
	£	£
Non-current assets	200,000	80,000
Investment in S Ltd	100,000	–
Net current assets	40,000	30,000
	340,000	110,000
Share capital	250,000	50,000
Retained earnings	90,000	60,000
	340,000	110,000

Prepare the consolidated balance sheet as at 31 March 20X2.

3   On 1 January 20X1 X Ltd purchased 75% of the ordinary share capital of Y Ltd when the retained earnings of Y Ltd stood at £240,000. At 31 December 20X1 the balance sheets of the two companies were as follows.

	X Ltd	Y Ltd
	£	£
Property, plant and equipment	800,000	400,000
Investment in Y Ltd	350,000	–
Net current assets	70,000	75,000
	1,220,000	475,000
Share capital	800,000	200,000
Retained earnings	420,000	275,000
	1,220,000	475,000

Prepare the consolidated balance sheet as at 31 December 20X1.

4   On 1 May 20X1 A Ltd acquired 100% of the share capital of B Ltd. At that date B Ltd's reserves
     stood at £480,000. On 30 April 20X2 the balance sheets of the two companies were as follows.

	A Ltd	B Ltd
	£	£
Property, plant and equipment	1,640,000	750,000
Investment in B Ltd	850,000	–
Net current assets	240,000	85,000
	2,730,000	835,000
Share capital	2,000,000	300,000
Retained earnings	730,000	535,000
	2,730,000	835,000

At 1 May 20X1 the book value of B Ltd's head office was £200,000 but its fair value was £240,000.
Buildings are to be depreciated at a rate of 2% per annum.

Prepare the consolidated balance sheet at 30 April 20X2.

5   A number of years ago C Ltd acquired 80% of the shares in D Ltd. At the date of acquisition the
     retained earnings of D Ltd stood at £200,000. The balance sheets of the two companies at 31
     March 20X2 were as follows.

	C Ltd	D Ltd
	£	£
Property, plant and equipment	1,000,000	625,000
Investment in D Ltd	460,000	–
	1,460,000	625,000
Current assets		
Inventory	60,000	30,000
Receivables	65,000 ~~80,000~~	50,000
Cash	10,000	5,000
	150,000	85,000
Total assets	1,610,000	710,000
Current liabilities	50,000	45,000 30,000
Net current assets	100,000	40,000
Net assets	1,560,000	665,000
Share capital	1,000,000	300,000
Retained earnings	560,000	365,000
	1,560,000	665,000

The following information is also relevant.

- Included in C Ltd's receivables is £15,000 due from D Ltd. This amount is also recorded as a payable in D Ltd's balance sheet.

- As at April 20X1 all goodwill had been fully written off.

Prepare the consolidated balance sheet as at 31 March 20X2.

6 On 1 January 20X0 F Ltd purchased 60% of the ordinary share capital of G Ltd. At that date G Ltd had retained earnings of £185,000. The balance sheets of the two companies at 31 December 20X2 were as follows.

	F Ltd £	G Ltd £
Property, plant and equipment	600,000	380,000
Investment in G Ltd	250,000	–
Net current assets	80,000	35,000
	930,000	415,000
Share capital	600,000	150,000
Retained earnings	330,000	265,000
	930,000	415,000

Prepare the consolidated balance sheet as a 31 December 20X2.

Only done as far as No 6.

Do remaining questions once gone over chapter in book again.

7   M Ltd acquired 80% of the ordinary share capital of N Ltd on 1 April 20X0 when N Ltd's retained earnings stood at £60,000. The balance sheets of the two companies at 31 March 20X2 are as follows.

	M Ltd		N Ltd	
	£	£	£	£
Non-current assets				
Property, plant and equipment		580,000		280,000
Investment in N Ltd		260,000		
		840,000		
Current assets				
Inventory	40,000		20,000	
Receivables	50,000		30,000	
Cash	5,000		2,000	
	95,000		52,000	
Total assets		935,000		332,000
Current liabilities		55,000		32,000
Net current assets		40,000		20,000
Net assets		880,000		300,000
Equity:				
Share capital		600,000		200,000
Retained earnings		280,000		100,000
		880,000		300,000

In January 20X2 M Ltd sold goods to N Ltd for £20,000. N Ltd has not yet paid for these goods and the balance due has been correctly recorded in each company's balance sheets

Prepare the consolidated balance sheet as at 31 March 20X2.

8 Paton Ltd has one subsidiary undertaking, MacNeal Ltd, which it acquired on 30 September 20X0. The balance sheet of MacNeal Ltd as at 30 September is set out below.

MACNEAL LIMITED
BALANCE SHEET AS AT 30 SEPTEMBER 20X0

	£'000	£'000
Non-current assets		4,844
Current assets	3,562	
Current liabilities	1,706	
Net current assets		1,856
Long-term loan		(1,900)
		4,800
Equity		
Called up share capital		1,200
Share premium		800
Retained earnings		2,800
		4,800

You have been given the following further information.

a) The share capital of MacNeal Ltd consists of ordinary shares of £1 each.

b) Paton Ltd acquired 900,000 shares in MacNeal Ltd on 30 September 20X0 at a cost of £5,000,000.

c) The fair value of the non-current assets of MacNeal Ltd at 30 September 20X0 was £5,844,000. The revaluation has not been reflected in the books of MacNeal Ltd.

Task

Calculate the goodwill on consolidation that arose on the acquisition of MacNeal Ltd on 30 September 20X0.

9   You have been asked to assist in the preparation of the consolidated accounts of the Norman Group. Set out below are the balance sheets of Norman Ltd and Saxon Ltd for the year ended 31 March 20X3.

BALANCE SHEETS AS AT 31 MARCH 20X3

	Norman Ltd £'000	Saxon Ltd £'000
Non-current assets:		
Property, plant and equipment +400 Revaluation	12,995	1,755
Investment in Saxon Ltd	1,978	–
	14,973	1,755
Current assets:		
Inventory	3,586	512
Trade and other receivables	2,193	382
Cash and cash equivalents	84	104
	5,863	998
Total assets	20,836	2,753
Current liabilities:		
Trade and other payables	1,920	273
Tax liabilities	667	196
	2,587	469
Net current assets	3,276	529
Long-term loan	–	400
Total liabilities	2,587	869
Net assets	18,249	1,884
Share capital	2,000	1,000
Share premium	–	200
Retained earnings Impairment	16,249	684
Revaluation 400		
	18,249	1,884

Further information

a)   The share capital of both Norman Ltd and Saxon Ltd consists of ordinary shares of £1 each. There have been no changes to the balances of share capital and share premium during the year. No dividends were paid by Saxon Ltd during the year.

b)   Norman Ltd acquired 750,000 shares in Saxon Ltd on 31 March 20X2.

c)   At 31 March 20X2 the balance on the retained earnings reserve of Saxon Ltd was £424,000.

d)   The fair value of the property, plant and equipment of Saxon Ltd at 31 March 20X2 was £2,047,000 as compared with their book value of £1,647,000. The revaluation has not been reflected in the books of Saxon Ltd. (Ignore any depreciation implications.)

e)   Goodwill arising on consolidation is reviewed for impairment at each year end. The directors estimate that by 31 March 20X3 goodwill had suffered an impairment loss of 10% of its original value.

Task

Prepare the consolidated balance sheet of Norman Ltd and its subsidiary as at 31 March 20X3.

10 Fertwrangler Ltd has one subsidiary, Voncarryon Ltd, which it acquired on 1 April 20X2. The balance sheet of Voncarryon Ltd as at 31 March 20X3 is set out below.

VONCARRYON LTD
BALANCE SHEET AS AT 31 MARCH 20X3

	£'000
Non-current assets + 400 fewdluchi	3,855
Current assets	4,961
Total assets	8,816
Current liabilities	2,546
Long term loan	1,500
Total liabilities	4,046
Net assets	4,770
Equity	
Share capital	2,000
Share premium	1,000
Retained earnings	1,770
	4,770

Further information

a) The share capital of Voncarryon Ltd consists of ordinary shares of £1 each. There have been no changes to the balances of share capital and share premium during the year. No dividends were paid by Voncarryon Ltd during the year.

b) Fertwrangler acquired 1,200,000 shares in Voncarryon Ltd on 1 April 20X2 at a cost of £3,510,000.

c) At 1 April 20X2 the balance on the retained earnings reserve of Voncarryon Ltd was £1,350,000.

d) The fair value of the non-current assets of Voncarryon Ltd at 1 April 20X2 was £4,455,000. The book value of the assets at 1 April 20X2 was £4,055,000. The revaluation has not been reflected in the books of Voncarryon Ltd.

e) Goodwill arising on consolidation had suffered an impairment loss of 10% of its original cost by 31 March 20X3.

f) At 31 March 20X3 the balance on the retained earnings reserve of Fertwrangler Ltd was £5,610,000.

Tasks

a) Calculate the goodwill figure relating to the acquisition of Voncarryon Ltd that will appear in the consolidated balance sheet of Fertwrangler Ltd as at 31 March 20X3.

b) Calculate the minority interest figure that will appear in the consolidated balance sheet of Fertwrangler Ltd at 31 March 20X3.

c) Calculate the balance on the consolidated retained earnings reserve that will appear in the consolidated balance sheet of Fertwrangler Ltd at 31 March 20X3.

d) Draft notes to reply to the following questions from one of the directors of Fertwrangler Ltd:

i) We are considering the purchase of a 40% interest in another company, Triumphara Ltd. Triumphara Ltd will not be a subsidiary, because we will not have a large enough shareholding to exercise control. However, it will be a very significant investment and we hope to play an active part in the affairs and policy decisions of the company.

1) What is an associate and will the investment in Triumphara Ltd fall within this category?

2) How should the investment be treated in the consolidated financial statements?

ii) Since the balance sheet date Fertwrangler Ltd has begun to sell goods to its subsidiary, Voncarryon Ltd. The two companies have never previously traded with each other.

Could you explain the way in which the inter-company sales will be treated in the consolidated financial statements?

chapter 11:
GROUP ACCOUNTS – FURTHER ASPECTS

1 P Ltd has owned 7,000 of the 10,000 ordinary shares in S Ltd since 1 April 20X0. The income statements for each company for the year ended 31 March 20X2 are given below.

	P Ltd £	S Ltd £
Revenue	460,000	221,000
Cost of sales	270,000	132,000
Gross profit	190,000	89,000
Operating expenses	87,000	43,000
Profit from operations	103,000	46,000
Investment income	7,000	–
Profit before tax	110,000	46,000
Tax	30,000	12,000
Profit for the year	80,000	34,000

Prepare the consolidated income statement for the year ended 31 March 20X2.

2 A Ltd acquired 60% of the share capital B Ltd a number of years ago. The income statement for each company for the year ended 30 April 20X2 are given below.

	A Ltd £	B Ltd £
Revenue	694,000	372,000
Cost of sales	416,000	223,000
Gross profit	278,000	149,000
Operating expenses	174,000	75,000
Profit from operations	104,000	74,000
Tax	26,000	19,000
Profit for the year	78,000	55,000

During the year A Ltd sold goods to B Ltd for £120,000. None of these goods remained in inventory at 30 April 20X2.

Prepare the consolidated income statement for the year ended 30 April 20X2.

3   C Ltd purchased 60% of the shares in D Ltd a number of years ago. The income statements for
    each company for the year ended 31 December 20X1 are given below.

	C Ltd £	D Ltd £
Revenue	386,000	147,000
Cost of sales	(250,000)	(95,000)
Gross profit	136,000	52,000
Operating expenses	(77,000)	(29,000)
Investment income	3,000	–
Profit before tax	62,000	23,000
Tax	(16,000)	(6,000)
Profit for the year	46,000	17,000

You are also given the following information.

– During the year to 31 December 20X1 D Ltd made sales to C Ltd totalling £50,000.
    None of the goods were still in inventory at the year end.

Prepare a consolidated income statement for the year ended 31 December 20X1.

4   Explain the equity method of accounting for associates in the balance sheet and income statement.
    Why is this method used for accounting for associates?

5   Gilbert Ltd, which has one wholly owned subsidiary, acquired 25% of the share capital of Charlotte
    Ltd on 1 April 20X1 when the retained earnings reserve of Charlotte Ltd was £40,000. The balance
    sheets and income statements of Gilbert Ltd and its subsidiary and Charlotte Ltd are given below.

BALANCE SHEETS AT 31 MARCH 20X2

	Gilbert group £	Charlotte Ltd £
Non-current assets		
Property, plant and equipment	410,000	82,000
Investment in Charlotte Ltd	24,000	–
	434,000	82,000
Current assets		
Inventory	61,000	16,000
Trade and other receivables	66,000	20,000
Cash	8,000	4,000
	135,000	40,000
Total assets	569,000	122,000
Current liabilities:		
Trade and other payables	102,000	25,000
Net current assets	33,000	15,000
Net assets	467,000	97,000
Equity		
Share capital	300,000	40,000
Retained earnings	167,000	57,000
	467,000	97,000

INCOME STATEMENTS FOR THE YEAR ENDED 31 MARCH 20X2

	Gilbert group £	Charlotte Ltd £
Revenue	410,000	80,000
Cost of sales	287,000	38,000
Gross profit	123,000	42,000
Operating expenses	84,000	21,000
Profit before tax	39,000	21,000
Tax	12,000	4,000
Profit for the year	27,000	17,000

Prepare the consolidated income statement for the year ended 31 March 20X2 and the consolidated balance sheet at that date for the Gilbert group, including its associate Charlotte Ltd according to the equity method of accounting.

6   Various plc has many subsidiaries. One of these, Odd Ltd, is a property development company; the rest of the group consists of a chain of furniture shops. The directors believe that the consolidated financial statements of the group would be misleading if Odd Ltd were to be included in the consolidation.

Can Odd Ltd be excluded from the consolidated financial statements of the Various Group?

7   The directors of Animalets are considering the following two options.

a)   The purchase of 30% of the share capital in Superpet, which would give the directors of Animalets influence over Superpet

or

b)   The purchase of 75% of the share capital in Superpet, which would give the directors of Animalets control over Superpet

Explain briefly how these two different options would be accounted for in the consolidated income statement and balance sheet of the Animalets Group.

PRACTICE EXAM 1

HAYDN PLC

These tasks were set by the AAT in December 2005.

Time allowed: 3 hours plus 15 minutes' reading time

This examination paper is in TWO sections.

You are reminded that competence must be achieved in EACH section. You should therefore attempt and aim to complete EVERY task in EACH section.

You are advised to spend approximately 125 minutes on Section 1 and 55 minutes on Section 2.

All essential workings should be included within your answers, where appropriate.

SECTION 1 (Suggested time allowance: 125 minutes)

This section is in three parts.

Part A

You should spend about 40 minutes on this part.

DATA

Haydn plc has one subsidiary, Seek Ltd, which was acquired on 1 October 20X4. The balance sheets of Haydn plc and Seek Ltd as at 30 September 20X5 are set out below.

	Haydn plc £'000	Seek Ltd £'000
Non-current assets:		
Property, plant and equipment	88,301	45,523
Investment in Seek Ltd	39,500	-
	127,801	45,523
Current assets:		
Inventories	25,205	6,861
Trade and other receivables	9,147	4,725
Cash and cash equivalents	401	1,028
	34,753	12,614
Total assets	162,554	58,137
Current liabilities:		
Trade and other payables	11,669	5,002
Accruals	2,984	991
Tax liabilities	1,832	714
	16,485	6,707
Net current assets	18,268	5,907
Non-current liabilities:		
Long-term loan	50,000	7,000
Total liabilities	66,485	13,707
Net assets	96,069	44,430
Equity:		
Share capital	30,000	5,000
Share premium	20,000	2,000
Retained earnings	46,069	37,430
Total equity	96,069	44,430

You have been given the following further information.

- The share capital of Seek Ltd consists of ordinary shares of £1 each. There have been no changes to the balances of share capital and share premium during the year. No dividends were paid or proposed by Seek Ltd during the year.

- Haydn plc acquired 3,000,000 shares in Seek Ltd on 1 October 20X4.

- At 1 October 20X4 the balance on the retained earnings reserve was £32,550,000.

- The fair value of the property, plant and equipment of Seek Ltd at 1 October 20X4 was £42,500,000. The book value of the property, plant and equipment at 1 October 20X4 was £38,500,000. The revaluation has not been recorded in the books of Seek Ltd. (Ignore any effect on the depreciation for the year.)

- The directors of Haydn plc consider that the goodwill in the consolidated financial statements has an indefinite economic life and that this can be demonstrated. They also believe that the goodwill is capable of continued measurement.

Task 1.1

Prepare the consolidated balance sheet of Haydn plc and its subsidiary as at 30 September 20X5.

Task 1.2

Advise the directors of Haydn plc on the accounting treatment of the goodwill in the consolidated financial statements.

Note. Your answer should make reference to relevant accounting standards.

Part B

You should spend about 55 minutes on this part.

DATA

The financial accountant of Moatsart Ltd is away from work due to ill health. You have been asked to take over the preparation of the financial statements of Moatsart Ltd for the year ended 30 September 20X5. An extended trial balance of the company as at 30 September has been produced by the accountant, but some of the balances need to be adjusted. The extended trial balance is on the following page.

Further information is as follows.

- All of the operations are continuing operations.

- The authorised share capital of the company consists of 20,000,000 ordinary shares with a nominal value of £1.

- At the beginning of the year the issued share capital was 8,000,000 ordinary shares. At the end of the year another 2,000,000 ordinary shares were issued at a price of £1.50 per share. This issue of shares has not been accounted for in the ledger accounts in the extended trial balance.

- The closing inventory at 30 September 20X5 was £8,731,000.

- Property, plant and equipment that had cost £2,300,000 and had accumulated depreciation of £1,250,000 was sold at the end of the year for £1,500,000 cash. The sale has not been accounted for in the ledger accounts in the extended trial balance.

- The corporation tax charge for the year has been calculated as £3,948,000.

- Interest on the long-term loan has been paid for six months of the year. No adjustment has been made for the interest due for the final six months of the year. Interest is charged on the loan at a rate of 8% per annum.

- No final dividend is proposed.

Task 1.3

Make the necessary journal entries as a result of the further information given above.

Notes.

1   You do not need to give any dates or narratives, but must show account names
2   You must show any workings relevant to these adjustments
3   Ignore any effect of these adjustments on the tax charge for the year given above

MOATSART LTD
EXTENDED TRIAL BALANCE AT 30 SEPTEMBER 20X5

Description	Trial balance Debit £'000	Trial balance Credit £'000	Adjustments Debit £'000	Adjustments Credit £'000	Income statement Debit £'000	Income statement Credit £'000	Balance sheet Debit £'000	Balance sheet Credit £'000
Purchases	37,543				37,543			
Sales		70,613				70,613		
Returns inward	2,372				2,372			
Returns outward		1,463				1,463		
Ord share capital		8,000 +2000						8,000 +2000
Share premium		3,000 +1,000						3,000 +1000
Revaluation reserve		2,500						2,500
Dividend paid	2,400				2,400			
Long-term loan		15,000						15,000
Inventory	7,454				7,454			
Non-current asset investments	4,000						4,000	
Admin expenses	7,115				7,115			
Distribution costs	12,386				12,386			
Prepayments	403						403	
Property, plant and equipment – cost	84,856 –2300						84,856 –2300	
Property, plant and equip – acc depn		26,422 –1250						26,422 –1250
Prov for doubtful debts		682						682
Trade receivables	8,754						8,754	
Trade payables		8,939						8,939
Accruals		642+600						642
Cash at bank	1,535+300–1500						1,535+300+1500	
Interest	600+600				600			
Retained earnings		32,157						32,157
Profit					2,206 +450			2,206 +450
Total	169,418	169,418			72,076	72,076	99,548	99,548

Gain on Disposal I/S

Tax Liability   450   3948

Tax Payable Exp. I/S   3948

Inventories

3948   3948
8731   8731   8731   8731

Task 1.4

a)   Draft an income statement for Moatsart Ltd for the year ended 30 September 20X5.
b)   Draft a balance sheet for Moatsart Ltd as at 30 September 20X5.

DATA

The directors of Moatsart Ltd are interested in the principles to be followed in selecting accounting policies for the company.

Task 1.5

a)   IAS 1 identifies two underlying assumptions (or concepts) of going concern and accruals that are fundamentally important to the preparation of financial statements and to the selection of accounting policies. Explain these two assumptions (or concepts).

b)   According to IAS 8, how should an entity decide what accounting policies should be adopted?

Part C

You should spend about 30 minutes on this part.

DATA

You have been asked to prepare a reconciliation between cash flows from operating activities and operating profit and to interpret the cash flow statement for Bateoven Ltd for the year ended 30 September 20X5. The balance sheet and cash flow statement of Bateoven Ltd are set out below.

Bateoven Ltd
Balance sheet at 30 September 20X5

	20X5 £'000	20X4 £'000
Non-current assets:		
Property, plant and equipment	23,814	18,507
Current assets:		
Inventories	3,670	3,162
Trade receivables	1,777	1,306
Cash and cash equivalents	93	1,401
	5,540	5,869
Total assets	29,354	24,376
Current liabilities:		
Trade payables	646	975
Tax liabilities	1,923	1,284
	2,569	2,259
Net current assets	2,971	3,610
Non-current assets:		
Long-term loan	9,100	5,000
Total liabilities	11,669	7,259
Net assets	17,685	17,117
Equity:		
Share capital	8,000	5,000
Share premium	4,000	2,000
Retained earnings	5,685	10,117
Total equity	17,685	17,117

Bateoven Ltd
Cash flow statement for the year ended 30 September 20X5

	£'000	£'000
Net cash from operating activities		730
Investing activities		
Purchase of property, plant and equipment	9,138	
Net cash used in operating activities		(9,138)
Financing activities		
Issue of equity capital	5,000	
Increase in long term loan	4,100	
Dividends paid	(2,000)	
Net cash from financing activities		7,100
Net decrease in cash and cash equivalents		(1,308)
Cash and cash equivalents at 1 October 20X4		1,401
Cash and cash equivalents at 30 September 20X5		93

Further information is as follows.

■ The profit from operations for the year ended 30 September 20X5 was £312,000. This was after depreciation of £3,570,000 was charged.

■ All sales and purchases were on credit. Other expenses were paid for in cash.

■ The interest expense for the year ended 30 September 20X5 was £560,000 and the tax expense was £1,923,000.

Task 1.6

Provide a reconciliation of profit from operations to net cash from operating activities for Bateoven Ltd for the year ended 30 September 20X5.

Task 1.7

Draft a letter to the directors of Bateoven Ltd commenting on the sources and uses of cash during the year ended 30 September 20X5 as indicated by the cash flow statement.

SECTION 2 (Suggested time allowance: 55 minutes)

DATA

John Brams is a shareholder of Ma Leer Ltd. He has obtained some ratios that are based on the financial statements of the company for the last two years. He is interested in how the directors have managed the business in the past year and in the company's financial performance. You have been asked to explain how the ratios were calculated and to analyse the financial performance of the company using the ratios computed. The ratios John has obtained are set out below.

Ratio	20X5	20X4
Return on capital employed	15%	19%
Net profit ratio	20%	22%
Gross profit ratio	46%	42%
Expenses ratio	26%	24%
Asset turnover (based on net assets)	0.75	0.86
Inventory turnover in days (inventory turnover period based on cost of sales)	93 days	71 days
Receivables turnover in days (receivables payment period)	54 days	47 days
Payables turnover in days (payables payment period based on cost of sales)	25 days	29 days

Task 2.1

Prepare a report for John Brams that includes the following.

a)   the formulae used to calculate each of the ratios

b)   a statement of whether the ratios have, in your opinion, improved or deteriorated in 20X5 when compared with 20X4, along with your reasons for thinking so

c)   your comments based on the overall change in financial performance of Ma Leer Ltd over the two years based on your analysis of the ratios and the relationship between them.

Task 2.2

a)   Explain how the use of financial information in Task 2.1 illustrates the objective of financial statements.

b)   Give TWO examples of other classes of user who might be interested in the information in financial statements. Explain what they might use this information for.

PRACTICE EXAM 2

TRUSTDAN PLC

These tasks were set by the AAT in June 2006.

Time allowed: 3 hours plus 15 minutes' reading time

This examination paper is in TWO sections.

You are reminded that competence must be achieved in EACH section. You should therefore attempt and aim to complete EVERY task in EACH section.

You are advised to spend approximately 125 minutes on Section 1 and 55 minutes on Section 2.

All essential workings should be included within your answers, where appropriate.

SECTION 1 (Suggested time allowance: 125 minutes)

This section is in four parts.

Part A

You should spend about 40 minutes on this part.

DATA

Trustdan plc has one subsidiary undertaking, Isold Ltd which was acquired on 1 April 20X5. The balance sheets of Trustdan plc and Isold Ltd as at 31 March 20X6 are set out on the next page.

Balance sheets as at 31 March 20X6

	Trustdan plc £'000	Isold Ltd £'000
Non-current assets		
Property, plant and equipment	75,107	32,637
Investment in Isold Ltd	28,000	-
	103,107	32,637
Current assets		
Inventories	28,273	7,663
Trade and other receivables	11,508	5,154
Receivable from Isold Ltd	3,000	
Cash and cash equivalents	2,146	68
	44,927	12,885
Total assets	148,034	45,522
Current liabilities		
Trade and other payables	(14,854)	(2,914)
Payable to Trustdan plc	-	(3,000)
Tax liabilities	(6,230)	(108)
	(21,084)	(6,022)
Net current assets	23,843	6,863
Non-current liabilities		
Long-term loan	(40,000)	(5,000)
Total liabilities	(61,084)	(11,022)
Net assets	86,950	34,500
EQUITY		
Share capital	35,000	10,000
Share premium account	15,000	2,000
Retained earnings	36,950	22,500
Total equity	86,950	34,500

You have been given the following further information.

- The share capital of Isold Ltd consists of ordinary shares of £1 each. Each share carries one vote and there are no other voting rights other than those attaching to the ordinary shares. There have been no changes to the balances of share capital and share premium during the year. No dividends were paid or proposed by Isold Ltd during the year.

- Trustdan plc acquired 7,500,000 shares in Isold Ltd on 1 April 20X5.

- At 1 April 20X5 the balance of retained earnings of Isold Ltd was £17,056,000.

- The fair value of the property, plant and equipment of Isold Ltd at 1 April 20X5 was £26,800,000. The book value of the property, plant and equipment at 1 April 20X5 was £23,800,000. The revaluation has not been recorded in the books of Isold Ltd. (Ignore any effect on the depreciation for the year.)

- The directors of Trustdan plc have concluded that goodwill has not been impaired during the year.

Task 1.1

Prepare the consolidated balance sheet of Trustdan plc and its subsidiary undertaking as at 31 March 20X6.

Task 1.2

Prepare brief notes for the directors to answer the following questions.

a)   What is a 'business combination'?
b)   How is the acquirer in a business combination identified?
c)   Explain why Trustdan plc is the acquirer in the business combination of Trustdan plc and Isold Ltd.

Note: Your answer should make reference to relevant International Accounting Standards.

Part B

You should spend about 60 minutes on this part.

DATA

You have been asked to help prepare the financial statements of Tanhosier Ltd for the year ended 31 March 20X6. A trial balance of the company as at 31 March 20X6 and draft journal entries have been produced by an assistant. The trial balance is shown below.

Tanhosier Ltd
Trial Balance as at 31 March 20X6

	Debit £'000	Credit £'000
Sales		50,332
Purchases	29,778	
Property, plant and equipment – cost	59,088	
Property, plant and equipment – accumulated depreciation		25,486
Inventories as at 1 April 20X5	7,865	
Interest	200	
Accruals		426
Distribution costs	8,985	
Administrative expenses	7,039	
Retained earnings		23,457
Trade receivables	9,045	
Cash at bank	182	
8% bank loan repayable 20X9		5,000
Share capital		10,000
Share premium		5,000
Trade payables		2,481
	122,182	122,182

The proposed journal entries produced by the assistant are based on the following further information. These journal entries have not yet been incorporated in the trial balance.

- The share capital of the company consists of ordinary shares with a nominal value of £1. No dividends are to be paid for the current year.

- The sales figure in the trial balance includes the sales made on credit for April 20X6 amounting to £3,147,000.

- The inventories at the close of business on 31 March 20X6 cost £8,407,000. Included in this figure are inventories that cost £480,000, but which can only be sold for £180,000.

- Transport costs of £157,000 relating to March 20X6 are not included in the accounts in the trial balance as the invoice was received after the year end.

- Interest on the bank loan for the last six months of the year has not been included in the accounts in the trial balance.

- The corporation tax charge for the year has been calculated as £235,000.
- All of the operations are continuing operations.

Task 1.3

Look at the assistant's proposed journal entries below. Where necessary, correct the proposed entries by crossing through errors and writing in your corrections.

			£'000	£'000
1.	DR	Trade receivables	3,147	
	CR	Sales		3,147
2.	DR	Inventory (Balance Sheet)	8,407	
	CR	Inventory (Income Statement)		8,407
3.	DR	Income statement	157	
	CR	Current liabilities		157
4.	DR	Interest payable	400	
	CR	Interest		400
5.	DR	Taxation	235	
	CR	Taxation payable		235

Task 1.4

a) Draft the income statement for Tanhosier Ltd for the year ended 31 March 20X6.
b) Draft the balance sheet for Tanhosier Ltd as at 31 March 20X6.

DATA

The directors of Tanhosier Ltd are about to undertake the development of a new product. They expect the costs of development to be significant and are concerned at the impact that this might have on their financial statements.

You have been asked to prepare notes to deal with the following queries of the directors.

Task 1.5

a) What is an intangible asset?

b) What would have to be demonstrated by Tanhosier Ltd before an intangible asset arising from development is recognised as an intangible asset in the financial statements?

Part C

You should spend about 25 minutes on this part.

DATA

For the year ended 31 March 20X6 you have been asked to prepare:

- a reconciliation between profit from operations and net cash from operating activities
- a cash flow statement for Lowandgrim Ltd.

The income statement and balance sheet of Lowandgrim Ltd are set out below.

Lowandgrim Ltd
Income Statement for the year ended 31 March 20X6

Continuing Operations

	£'000
Revenue	27,821
Cost of sales	(13,632)
Gross profit	14,189
Gain on disposal of property, plant and equipment	274
Distribution costs	(6,093)
Administrative expenses	(4,156)
Profit from operations	4,214
Finance costs – interest on loan	(480)
Profit before tax	3,734
Tax	(821)
Profit for the period from continuing operations attributable to equity holders	2,913

Lowandgrim Ltd
Balance Sheet as at 31 March

	20X6 £'000	20X5 £'000
Non-current assets		
Property, plant and equipment	38,710	30,370
Current assets		
Inventories	4,637	4,205
Trade receivables	5,043	4,773
Cash and cash equivalents	488	81
	10,168	9,059
Total assets	48,878	39,429
Current liabilities		
Trade payables	(3,523)	(3,146)
Tax liabilities	(821)	(662)
	(4,344)	(3,808)
Net current assets	5,824	5,251
Non-current liabilities		
Bank loans	(6,000)	(4,000)
Total liabilities	(10,344)	(7,808)
Net assets	38,534	31,621
EQUITY		
Share capital	6,000	4,000
Share premium account	3,000	1,000
Retained earnings	29,534	26,621
Total equity	38,534	31,621

Further information

- The total depreciation charge for the year was £4,555,000.

- Property, plant and equipment costing £1,022,000 with accumulated depreciation of £487,000 was sold in the year.

- All sales and purchases were on credit. Other expenses were paid for in cash.

Task 1.6

Provide a note to the accounts showing the reconciliation of profit from operations to net cash from operating activities for Lowandgrim Ltd for the year ended 31 March 20X6.

Task 1.7

Prepare the cash flow statement for Lowandgrim Ltd for the year ended 31 March 20X6.

SECTION 2 (Suggested time allowance: 55 minutes)

DATA

Rachel Wagnor is a shareholder in Wring Ltd. She wishes to assess the efficiency and effectiveness of the management of the company. She has asked you to help her by analysing the financial statements of the company for the last two years. These are set out below.

Wring Ltd
Income Statements
for the year ended 31 March

	20X6 £'000	20X5 £'000
Continuing Operations		
Revenue	21,473	19,882
Cost of sales	(9,878)	(9,543)
Gross profit	11,595	10,339
Distribution costs	(4,181)	(3,873)
Administrative expenses	(3,334)	(2,092)
Profit from operations	4,080	4,374
Finance costs	(350)	(350)
Profit before tax	3,730	4,024
Tax	(858)	(926)
Profit for the period from continuing operations attributable to equity holders	2,872	3,098

Wring Ltd
Balance Sheets as at 31 March

	20X6 £'000	20X5 £'000
Non-current assets		
Property, plant and equipment	27,781	26,125
Current assets		
Inventories	1,813	1,438
Trade receivables	3,000	1,906
Cash and cash equivalents	62	341
	4,875	3,685
Total assets	32,656	29,810
Current liabilities		
Trade and other payables	(1,235)	(1,193)
Tax liabilities	(858)	(926)
	(2,093)	(2,119)
Net current assets	2,782	1,566
Non-current liabilities		
Bank loans	(5,000)	(5,000)
Total liabilities	(7,093)	(7,119)
Net assets	25,563	22,691
EQUITY		
Share capital	5,000	5,000
Retained earnings	20,563	17,691
Total equity	25,563	22,691

Task 2.1

Prepare a report for Rachel Wagnor that includes:

a) the formulae that are used to calculate each of the following ratios:

  i)   gross profit ratio
  ii)   net profit ratio
  iii) inventories turnover in days (based on cost of sales)
  iv)   trade receivables turnover in days (trade receivables payment period)

b) a calculation of the above ratios for the two years

c) a comment on the relative performance of the company for the two years based on the ratios calculated and what this tells you about the company

d) ONE suggestion as to how the performance as indicated by each of the ratios might be improved.

Task 2.2

a) Set out the accounting equation and define the elements in the equation.
b) Briefly explain how profit for the year affects the elements in the accounting equation.

PRACTICE EXAM 3

HOWARDSEND LTD

These tasks were set by the AAT in December 2006.

Time allowed: 3 hours plus 15 minutes' reading time

This examination paper is in TWO sections.

You are reminded that competence must be achieved in EACH section. You should therefore attempt and aim to complete EVERY task in EACH section.

You are advised to spend approximately 125 minutes on Section 1 and 55 minutes on Section 2.

All essential workings should be included within your answers, where appropriate.

SECTION 1 (Suggested time allowance: 125 minutes)

This section is in three parts.

Part A

You should spend about 60 minutes on this part.

DATA

The directors of Howardsend Ltd have asked you to prepare the financial statements of the company for the year ended 30 September 20X6. An extended trial balance (ETB) as at 30 September 20X6 has been taken from the computerised accounting system. Some of the balances need to be adjusted. The ETB is on the next page.

ThanHOWARDSEND LTD
EXTENDED TRIAL BALANCE AS AT 30 SEPTEMBER 20X6

Description	Trial balance Debit £'000	Trial balance Credit £'000	Adjustments Debit £'000	Adjustments Credit £'000	Income statement Debit £'000	Income statement Credit £'000	Balance sheet Debit £'000	Balance sheet Credit £'000
Inventories at 1 October 20X5	7,158				7,158			
Administration expenses	9,086		90+79		9,176			
Interest	350		350		350			
Sales		54,177		57+214+350 / 1,382		54,177		
Accruals				79				214
Purchases	24,610		2403		24,610			
Allowance for doubtful receivables		53						53
Distribution costs	12,092		57+124		12,216			
Long-term loan		10,000						10,000
Ordinary share capital		8,000						8,000
Share premium		1,000						1,000
Cash at bank	579		2000				579	
Property, plant and equipment – cost	57,149						57,149	
Property, plant and equipment – accum depn		14,523						14,523
Returns inwards	356				356			
Returns outwards		203				203		
Trade receivables	6,600			2403			6,600	
Trade payables		2,577						2,577
Final dividend paid for 20X5	960						960	
Interim dividend paid for 20X6	480						480	
Retained earnings		28,887						28,887
Profit for the year					514			514
TOTAL	119,420	119,420	214	214	54,380	54,380	65,768	65,768

Tax Payable
Revaluation Reserve

1382

2,080

91

ADDITIONAL DATA

- The share capital of the company consists of ordinary shares with a nominal value of £1.
- The directors propose a final dividend of 7p for the year ended 30 September 20X6.
- Credit purchases relating to September 20X6 amounting to £2,403,000 had not been entered into the accounts at the year end.
- An allowance for doubtful receivables is to be maintained at 2% of trade receivables.
- The inventories at the close of business on 30 September 20X6 cost £8,134,000.
- The company employed an advertising agency during the year to promote a new product. The cost of the advertising campaign was agreed at £57,000, but no invoices have yet been received for this expense and no adjustment has been made for it in the ETB. This is to be included in distribution costs.
- Interest on the long-term loan for the last six months of the year has not been included in the accounts in the trial balance. Interest is charged at 7% per annum.
- The corporation tax charge for the year has been calculated as £1,382,000.
- Land that had cost £9,600,000 has been revalued by professional valuers at £11,600,000.
- No adjustment has yet been made in the balances in the ETB. The revaluation is to be included in the financial statements for the year ended 30 September 20X6.
- All the operations are continuing operations.

Task 1.1

Make the necessary journal entries as a result of the additional information given above.

Task 1.2

a)   Draft the income statement for Howardsend Ltd for the year ended 30 September 20X6.

b)   Draft the balance sheet for Howardsend Ltd as at 30 September 20X6.

c)   Briefly explain why confidentiality is necessary in the preparation of the financial statements of Howardsend Ltd. Give an example of how confidentiality is assured in the preparation of financial statements.

Note: Additional notes and disclosures are not required.

Part B

You should spend about 35 minutes on this part.

DATA

Klarke plc acquired a subsidiary undertaking, Cameroon Ltd on 1 October 20X5. The balance sheets of Klarke plc and Cameroon Ltd as at 30 September 20X6 are set out below.

Balance sheets as at 30 September 20X6

	Klarke plc £'000	Cameroon Ltd £'000
Non-current assets		
Property, plant and equipment	53,181	36,762
Investment in Cameroon Ltd	29,000	
	82,181	36,762
Current assets		
Inventories	18,083	5,036
Trade and other receivables	9,514	4,997
Cash and cash equivalents	887	304
	28,484	10,337
Total assets	110,665	47,099
Current liabilities		
Trade and other payables	(7,437)	(3,042)
Tax liabilities	(4,003)	(687)
	(11,440)	(3,729)
Net current assets	17,044	6,608
Non-current liabilities		
Long term loan	(35,000)	(8,000)
Total liabilities	(46,440)	(11,729)
Net assets	64,225	35,370
EQUITY		
Share capital	20,000	5,000
Share premium account	10,000	2,000
Retained earnings	34,225	28,370
Total equity	64,225	35,370

ADDITIONAL DATA

- The share capital of Cameroon Ltd consists of ordinary shares of £1 each. There have been no changes to the balances of share capital and share premium during the year. No dividends were paid or proposed by Cameroon Ltd during the year.

- Klarke plc acquired 3,000,000 shares in Cameroon Ltd on 1 October 20X5.

- At 1 October 20X5 the balance of retained earnings of Cameroon Ltd was £24,700,000.

- The fair value of the non-current assets of Cameroon Ltd at 1 October 20X5 was £37,000,000. The book value of the non-current assets at 1 October 20X5 was £33,000,000. The revaluation has not been recorded in the books of Cameroon Ltd (ignore any effect on the depreciation for the year). There were no other differences between the book value and the fair value of the other assets and liabilities of Cameroon Ltd at the date of acquisition.

- The directors have concluded that goodwill on the acquisition of Cameroon Ltd has been impaired during the year. They estimate that the impairment loss amounts to 20% of the goodwill.

Task 1.3

Calculate the following figures relating to the acquisition of Cameroon Ltd that will appear in the consolidated balance sheet of Klarke plc as at 30 September 20X6:

a)   The goodwill arising on acquisition
b)   The minority interest
c)   The consolidated retained earnings of the group.

DATA

According to IAS 36 the loss on impairment of an asset is calculated by taking into account the carrying value of the asset and its recoverable amount.

Task 1.4

a)   Explain what is meant by the 'carrying value' and 'recoverable amount' of an asset.
b)   How is the loss on impairment of goodwill calculated?
c)   How is the loss on impairment treated in the financial statements?

Part C

You should spend about 30 minutes on this part.

DATA

You have been asked to prepare a reconciliation between profit from operations and net cash from operating activities and to prepare a cash flow statement for Kenadie Ltd for the year ended 30 September 20X6. The income statement and balance sheet of Kenadie Ltd are set out below.

Kenadie Ltd
Income statement for the year ended 30 September 20X6

	£'000
Continuing Operations	
Revenue	31,461
Cost of sales	(16,304)
Gross profit	15,157
Loss on disposal of property, plant and equipment	(183)
Distribution costs	(5,663)
Administrative expenses	(3,681)
Profit from operations	5,630
Finance costs – interest on loan	(800)
Profit before tax	4,830
Tax	(919)
Profit for the period from continuing operations attributable to equity holders	3,911

Kenadie Ltd
Balance sheets as at 30 September

	20X6 £'000	20X5 £'000
Non-current assets		
Property, plant and equipment	29,882	19,100
Current assets		
Inventories	4,837	4,502
Trade and other receivables	5,244	4,978
Cash and cash equivalents	64	587
	10,145	10,067
Total assets	40,027	29,167
Current liabilities		
Trade and other payables	(3,038)	(2,954)
Tax liabilities	(919)	(854)
	(3,957)	(3,808)
Net current assets	6,188	6,259
Non-current liabilities		
Bank loans	(10,000)	(7,000)
Total liabilities	(13,957)	(10,808)
Net assets	26,070	18,359
EQUITY		
Share capital	8,000	5,000
Share premium account	2,500	1,000
Retained earnings Note	15,570	12,359
Total equity	26,070	18,359

Note to the accounts: Retained earnings

	£'000
Balance at 1 October 20X5	12,359
Dividends paid	(700)
Profit for the year	3,911
Balance at 30 September 20X6	15,570

ADDITIONAL DATA

- The total depreciation charge for the year was £2,172,000.
- Property, plant and equipment costing £1,103,000, with accumulated depreciation of £411,000, was sold in the year.
- All sales and purchases were on credit. Other expenses were paid for in cash.

Task 1.5

Provide a note to the accounts showing the reconciliation of profit from operations to net cash from operating activities for Kenadie Ltd for the year ended 30 September 20X6.

Task 1.6

Prepare the cash flow statement for Kenadie Ltd for the year ended 30 September 20X6.

SECTION 2 (Suggested time allowance: 55 minutes)

DATA

Bonnie Tair is a shareholder in Labor Ltd. She wishes to assess the profitability and effectiveness of the company. She has asked you to assist her by analysing the financial statements of the company for the last two years that are set out below.

Labor Ltd
Income Statements for the year ended 30 September

	20X6 £'000	20X5 £'000
Continuing Operations		
Revenue	37,384	36,103
Cost of sales	(21,458)	(21,120)
Gross profit	15,926	14,983
Distribution costs	(6,142)	(5,932)
Administrative expenses	(6,158)	(4,574)
Profit from operations	3,626	4,477
Finance costs	(639)	(960)
Profit before tax	2,987	3,517
Tax	(687)	(809)
Profit for the period from continuing operations attributable to equity holders	2,300	2,708

Labor Ltd
Balance sheets as at 30 September

	20X6 £'000	20X5 £'000
Non-current assets		
Property, plant and equipment	23,366	25,229
Current assets		
Inventories	4,461	4,520
Trade receivables	3,115	3,008
Cash and cash equivalents	213	191
	7,789	7,719
Total assets	31,155	32,948
Current liabilities		
Trade and other payables	(2,789)	(2,760)
Tax liabilities	(687)	(809)
	(3,476)	(3,569)
Net current assets	4,313	4,150
Non-current liabilities		
Bank loans	(8,000)	(12,000)
Total liabilities	(11,476)	(15,569)
Net assets	19,679	17,379
EQUITY		
Share capital	3,000	3,000
Retained earnings	16,679	14,379
Total equity	19,679	17,379

Task 2.1

Prepare a letter for Bonnie Tair that includes:

a) the formulae that are used to calculate each of the following ratios:

i) return on capital employed
ii) net profit ratio
iii) gross profit ratio
iv) asset turnover (based on capital employed)

b) a calculation of each of the above ratios for the two years

c) i) an explanation of the ratios

ii) a comment on the relative performance and effectiveness of the company for the two years based on the ratios calculated

iii) a comment on what this tells you about the performance and effectiveness of the company over the two years

d) a comment on the overall change in financial performance and effectiveness of the company over the two years.

Task 2.2

a) What are the elements that appear in financial statements according to the Framework for the Preparation and Presentation of Financial Statements?

b) Define the elements that appear in the balance sheet of a company in accordance with the definitions in the Framework for the Preparation and Presentation of Financial Statements.

PRACTICE EXAM 4

RICSCHTEIN LTD

These tasks were set by the AAT in June 2007.

Time allowed: 3 hours plus 15 minutes' reading time

This examination paper is in TWO sections.

You must show competence in BOTH sections. So, try to complete EVERY task in BOTH sections.

You should spend about 125 minutes on Section 1 and 55 minutes on Section 2.

You should include all your workings and essential calculations in your answers.

SECTION 1 (Suggested time allowance: 125 minutes)

This section is in three parts.

Part A

You should spend about 60 minutes on this part.

DATA

You have been asked to help prepare the financial statements of Ricschtein Ltd for the year ended 31 March 20X7. The company's trial balance as at 31 March 20X7 is shown below.

Ricschtein Ltd
Trial balance as at 31 March 20X7

	Debit £'000	Credit £'000
Share capital		7,000 +3,000
Trade payables		2,236
Property, plant and equipment – cost	39,371	
Property, plant and equipment – accumulated depreciation		13,892
Trade receivables	4,590	
Accruals		207
7% bank loan repayable 20Y2		14,000
Cash at bank	423 –87	
Retained earnings		9,552
Interest	490 +490	
Sales		37,365
Purchases	22,157	
Returns inwards	641	
Returns outwards		408
Distribution costs	5,517	
Administrative expenses ***	3,904 +87-9	
Loss on business disposed of during the year	347	
Inventories as at 1April 20X6	6,120	
Final dividend for year ended 31 March 20X6	600	
Interim dividend for year ended 31 March 20X7	500	
	84,660	84,660

Prepayment   Dr. 9
Accrual   Cr. 490

Further information Tax   Dr. Expense 1,170   Cr. Accrual 1,170

- The share capital of the company consists of ordinary shares with a nominal value of £1.

- At the beginning of the year the issued share capital was 7,000,000 ordinary shares. At the end of the year another 3,000,000 ordinary shares were issued at a price of £3.00 per share. Due to a misunderstanding about the date of the share issue, this has not been accounted for in the ledger accounts in the trial balance.

- The inventories at the close of business on 31 March 20X7 cost £7,304,000.

- Administrative expenses of £87,000 relating to February 20X7 have not been included in the trial balance.

- The company paid £36,000 insurance costs in June 20X6, which covered the period from 1 July 20X6 to 30 June 20X7. This was included in the administrative expenses in the trial balance.

- Interest on the bank loan for the last six months of the year has not been included in the accounts in the trial balance.

- The corporation tax charge for the year has been calculated as £1,170,000.

- The loss on a business disposed of during the year relates to a retail operation sold in the year. All of the other operations are continuing operations.

Task 1.1

Make the necessary journal entries as a result of the further information given above.

Task 1.2

a)   Draft the income statement for Ricschtein Ltd for the year ended 31 March 20X7.
b)   Draft the balance sheet for Ricschtein Ltd as at 31 March 20X7.

ADDITIONAL DATA

Ricschtein Ltd purchases goods for resale. The Directors of the company would like you to clarify the accounting treatment of inventories and when to recognise revenue arising from the sale of goods. Answer the following queries of the Directors.

Task 1.3

a)   What are inventories in Ricschtein Ltd? How are inventories measured? What is included in the cost of inventories?

b)   What is revenue in Ricschtein Ltd? How should it be measured? When should revenue be recognised?

Note: Your answer should refer to relevant International Accounting Standards.

Part B

You should spend about 30 minutes on this part.

DATA

The Managing Director of Wraymand plc has asked you to prepare the income statement for the group. The company has one subsidiary undertaking, Blonk Ltd. The income statements of the two companies for the year ended 31 March 20X7 are set out below.

Income statements
for the year ended 31 March 20X7

	Wraymand plc £'000	Blonk Ltd £'000
Continuing operations		
Revenue	38,462	12,544
Cost of sales	(22,693)	(5,268)
Gross profit	15,769	7,276
Other income – dividend from Blonk Ltd	580	-
Distribution costs	(6,403)	(2,851)
Administrative expenses	(3,987)	(2,466)
Profit from operations	5,959	1,959
Finance costs	(562)	(180)
Profit before tax	5,397	1,779
Tax	(1,511)	(623)
Profit for the period from continuing operations attributable to equity holders	3,886	1,156

Further information

- Wraymand plc acquired 75% of the ordinary share capital of Blonk Ltd on 1 April 20X6.
- During the year Blonk Ltd sold goods which had cost £1,100,000 to Wraymand plc for £1,600,000. All of the goods had been sold by Wraymand plc by the end of the year.

when query £1.6 B take out.

Task 1.4

Draft a consolidated income statement for Wraymand plc and its subsidiary undertaking for the year ended 31 March 20X7.

Part C

You should spend about 35 minutes on this part.

DATA

You have been asked to prepare a cash flow statement for Goramsee Ltd for the year ended 31 March 20X7. You have also been asked to comment on the change in net cash from operating activities. A note on net cash from operating activities for the period that reconciles it with profit from operations has been prepared. The balance sheets of Goramsee Ltd for the past two years and the note on net cash from operating activities are set out below.

Goramsee Ltd
Balance sheets as at 31 March

		20X7 £'000	20X6 £'000
Non-current assets			
Property, plant and equipment		35,557	26,084
Current assets			
Inventories		5,048	3,872
Trade and other receivables		3,116	2,243
Cash and cash equivalents		-	539
		8,164	6,654
Total assets		43,721	32,738
Current liabilities			
Trade and other payables		(1,604)	(1,722)
Tax liabilities		(1,595)	(1,314)
Bank overdraft		(997)	-
		(4,196)	(3,036)
Net current assets		3,968	3,618
Non-current liabilities			
Bank loans		(8,000)	(6,000)
Total liabilities		(12,196)	(9,036)
Net assets		31,525	23,702
Equity			
Share capital		10,000	8,000
Share premium account		3,000	1,000
Retained earnings	Note 1	18,525	14,702
Total equity		31,525	23,702

Note 1: Retained earnings

	£'000
Balance at 1 April 20X6	14,702
Dividends paid	(960)
Profit for the year	4,783
Balance at 31 March 20X7	18,525

Further information:

- The total depreciation charge for the year was £4,217,000.

- Property, plant and equipment costing £1,037,000 with accumulated depreciation of £731,000 was sold in the year at a profit of £434,000.

Goramsee Ltd
Reconciliation of operating profit to net cash inflow from operating activities

	20X7 £'000	20X6 £'000
Profit from operations	6,938	5,721
Adjustments for:		
Depreciation	4,217	2,843
Gain on disposal of property, plant and equipment	(434)	(86)
Operating cash flows before movements in working capital	10,721	8,478
Increase in inventories	(1,176)	(102)
Increase in trade receivables	(873)	(85)
Increase/(Decrease) in trade payables	(118)	113
Cash generated by operations	8,554	8,404
Income taxes paid	(1,314)	(1,276)
Interest paid	(560)	(420)
Net cash from operating activities	6,680	6,708

Task 1.5

Prepare a cash flow statement for Goramsee Ltd for the year ended 31 March 20X7.

Task 1.6

Prepare a report for the Directors of Goramsee Ltd to explain the change in net cash from operating activities between 20X6 and 20X7.

SECTION 2 (Suggested time allowance: 55 minutes)

DATA

You have been asked by the Managing Director of Gariroads Ltd to advise the company on the feasibility of raising a loan to finance the expansion of its activities.

A meeting has already been held with the bank and they have been sent a copy of the financial statements of the company for the past two years. The Managing Director wants you to comment on the likelihood of the bank lending the company money on the basis of the financial position revealed in the financial statements alone.

You have been given the income statement and balance sheets of the company for the last two years. These are set out below.

Gariroads Ltd
Income statements for the year ended 31 March

	20X7 £'000	20X6 £'000
Continuing operations		
Revenue	20,562	18,973
Cost of sales	(11,309)	(9,676)
Gross profit	9,253	9,297
Distribution costs	(4,841)	(4,414)
Administrative expenses	(3,007)	(2,701)
Profit from operations	1,405	2,182
Finance costs – interest on bank loan	(800)	(480)
Profit before tax	605	1,702
Tax	(133)	(374)
Profit for the period from continuing operations attributable to equity holders	472	1,328

Gariroads Ltd
Balance sheets as at 31 March

	20X7 £'000	20X6 £'000
Non-current assets		
Property, plant and equipment	23,982	16,015
Current assets		
Inventories	4,012	2,463
Trade and other receivables	2,241	2,249
Cash and cash equivalents	84	1,485
	6,337	6,197
Total assets	30,319	22,212
Current liabilities		
Trade and other payables	(2,773)	(2,577)
Tax liabilities	(133)	(374)
	(2,906)	(2,951)
Net current assets	3,431	3,246
Non-current liabilities		
Bank loans	(14,000)	(6,000)
Total liabilities	(16,906)	(8,951)
Net assets	13,413	13,261
Equity		
Share capital	4,000	4,000
Retained earnings	9,413	9,261
Total equity	13,413	13,261

Task 2.1

Prepare a letter for the Managing Director of Gariroads that includes the following:

a)   a calculation of the following ratios of Gariroads Ltd for each of the two years:

   i)   current ratio
   ii)   quick ratio
   iii)   gearing ratio
   iv)   interest cover

b)   an explanation of the meaning of each ratio

c)   a comment on how the liquidity and financial position of Gariroads Ltd has changed over the two years based solely on the ratios calculated

d)   a conclusion, with reasons, as to whether it is likely that the bank will lend the company money based solely on the ratios calculated and their analysis.

Task 2.2

a) What is the objective of financial statements according to the IASB Framework for the Preparation and Presentation of Financial Statements?

b) Give TWO examples of users of financial statements and explain for what purpose they might use information in financial statements.

PRACTICE EXAM 5

BENARD LTD

These tasks were set by the AAT in December 2007.

Time allowed: 3 hours plus 15 minutes' reading time

This examination paper is in TWO sections.

You must show competence in BOTH sections. So, try to complete EVERY task in BOTH sections.

You should include all your workings and essential calculations in your answers.

You should spend about 125 minutes on Section 1 and 55 minutes on Section 2.

SECTION 1 (Suggested time allowance: 125 minutes)

This section is in three parts.

Part A

You should spend about 55 minutes on this part.

DATA

You have been asked to help prepare the financial statements of Benard Ltd for the year ended 31 October 20X7. The company's trial balance as at 31 October 20X7 is shown below.

Benard Ltd
Trial balance as at 31 October 20X7

	Debit £'000	Credit £'000
Share capital		12,000
Trade and other payables		3,348
Property, plant and equipment – cost	58,463	
Property, plant and equipment – accumulated depreciation		27,974
Trade and other receivables	6,690	
Accruals		387
7% bank loan repayable 20Y2		16,000
Cash at bank	1,184	
Retained earnings		12,345
Interest	560	
Sales		50,875
Purchases	35,245	
Returns inwards	678	
Returns outwards		453
Distribution costs	6,654	
Administrative expenses	4,152	
Inventories as at 1 November 20X6	8,456	
Final dividend for year ended 31 October 20X6	700	
Interim dividend for year ended 31 October 20X7	600	
	123,382	123,382

Further information

- The share capital of the company consists of ordinary shares with a nominal value of £1.
- The sales figure in the trial balance does not include the credit sales for October 20X7 of £3,564,000.
- The inventories at the close of business on 31 October 20X7 cost £9,786,000.
- Goods for resale costing £127,000 purchased on two months' credit in October 20X7 were returned to the supplier on 30 October 20X7. No entries have been made in the accounts in the trial balance.
- The company paid £48,000 insurance costs in June 20X7, which covered the period from 1 July 20X7 to 30 June 20X8. This was included in administrative expenses in the trial balance.
- Interest on the bank loan for the last six months of the year has not been included in the accounts in the trial balance.
- The corporation tax charge for the year has been calculated as £1,254,000.
- All of the operations are continuing operations.

Task 1.1

Make the necessary journal entries as a result of the further information given above.

Task 1.2

a) Draft the income statement for Benard Ltd for the year ended 31 October 20X7.
b) Draft the balance sheet for Benard Ltd as at 31 October 20X7.

Part B

You should spend about 45 minutes on this part.

DATA

The Managing Director of Dumyat plc has asked you to prepare the balance sheet for the group. Dumyat plc has one subsidiary undertaking, Devon Ltd. The balance sheets of the two companies as at 31 October 20X7 are set out below.

Balance sheets as at 31 October 20X7

	Dumyat plc £'000	Devon Ltd £'000
Non-current assets		
Property, plant and equipment	65,388	31,887 +300
Investment in Devon Ltd	26,000	
	91,388	31,887
Current assets		
Inventories	28,273	5,566
Trade and other receivables	11,508	5,154
Receivable from Devon Ltd	4,000	0
Cash and cash equivalents	2,146	68
	45,927	10,788
Total assets	137,315	42,675
Current liabilities		
Trade and other payables	(13,554)	(1,475)
Payable to Dumyat plc	0	(4,000)
Tax liabilities	(6,140)	(108)
	(19,694)	(5,583)
Net current assets	26,233	5,205
Non-current liabilities		
Long-term loans	(25,000)	(4,000)
Total liabilities	(44,694)	(9,583)
Net assets	92,621	33,092
Equity		
Share capital	25,000	12,000
Share premium	12,000	4,000
Retained earnings	55,621	17,092 +3,00
Total equity	92,621	33,092

You have been given the following further information.

- The share capital of Devon Ltd consists of ordinary shares of £1 each. Ownership of these shares carries voting rights in Devon Ltd. There have been no changes to the balances of share capital and share premium during the year. No dividends were paid or proposed by Devon Ltd during the year.

- Dumyat plc acquired 9,000,000 shares in Devon Ltd on 1 November 20X6.

- At 1 November 20X6 the balance of retained earnings of Devon Ltd was £12,052,000.

- The fair value of the non-current assets of Devon Ltd at 1 November 20X6 was £28,800,000. The book value of the non-current assets at 1 November 20X6 was £25,800,000. The revaluation has not been recorded in the books of Devon Ltd (ignore any effect on the depreciation for the year).

- The directors of Dumyat plc have concluded that goodwill has not been impaired during the year.

Task 1.3

Draft a consolidated balance sheet for Dumyat plc and its subsidiary undertaking as at 31 October 20X7.

Task 1.4

Prepare brief notes for the directors to answer the following questions.

a)   What is a 'business combination'?
b)   How is the acquirer in a business combination identified?
c)   Explain why Dumyat plc is the acquirer in a business combination.

Part C

You should spend about 25 minutes on this part.

DATA

For the year ended 31 October 20X7 you have been asked to prepare:

- a reconciliation between profit from operations and net cash from operating activities
- a cash flow statement for Lochnagar Ltd.

The balance sheets of Lochnagar Ltd for the past two years and the most recent income statement are set out below:

Lochnagar Ltd
Income statement for the year ended 31 October 20X7

	£'000
Continuing operations	
Revenue	22,400
Cost of sales	(12,320)
Gross profit	10,080
Gain on disposal of property, plant and equipment	224
Distribution costs	(4,704)
Administrative expenses	(2,240)
Profit from operations	3,360
Finance costs – interest on loans	(91)
Profit before tax	3,269
Tax	(1,344)
Profit for the period from continuing operations attributable to equity holders	1,925

Lochnagar Ltd
Balance sheets as at 31 October

	20X7 £'000	20X6 £'000
Non-current assets		
Property, plant and equipment	25,171	24,100
Current assets		
Inventories	3,696	2,464
Trade and other receivables	3,360	2,464
Cash and cash equivalents	0	129
	7,056	5,057
Total assets	32,227	29,157
Current liabilities		
Trade and other payables	(1,232)	(1,848)
Tax liability	(1,344)	(944)
Bank overdraft	(361)	0
	(2,937)	(2,792)
Net current assets	4,119	2,265
Non-current liabilities		
Bank loans	(1,300)	(800)
Total liabilities	(4,237)	(3,592)
Net assets	27,990	25,565
Equity		
Share capital	2,200	2,000
Share premium	800	500
Retained earnings	24,990	23,065
Total equity	27,990	25,565

Further information

- The total depreciation charge for the year was £3,545,000.

- Property, plant and equipment costing £976,000 with accumulated depreciation of £355,000 was sold in the year at a profit of £224,000.

- All sales and purchases were on credit. Other expenses were paid for in cash.

Task 1.5

Provide a reconciliation of profit from operations to net cash from operating activities for Lochnagar Ltd for the year ended 31 October 20X7.

Task 1.6

Prepare the cash flow statement for Lochnagar Ltd for the year ended 31 October 20X7.

SECTION 2 (Suggested time allowance: 55 minutes)

DATA

Sally Forth is a shareholder in Tay Ltd. She wishes to assess the efficiency and effectiveness of the management of the company. She has asked you to assist her by analysing the financial statements of the company for the last two years. The financial statements of Tay Ltd are set out below:

Tay Ltd
Income statements for the year ended 31 October

	20X7 £'000	20X6 £'000
Continuing operations		
Revenue	2,400	2,100
Cost of sales	(1,392)	(1,155)
Gross profit	1,008	945
Distribution costs	(540)	(472)
Administrative expenses	(240)	(315)
Profit from operations	228	158
Finance costs	(91)	(56)
Profit before tax	137	102
Tax	(44)	(22)
Profit for the period from continuing operations attributable to equity holders	93	80

Tay Ltd
Balance sheets as at 31 October

	20X7 £'000	20X6 £'000
Non-current assets		
Property,plant and equipment	4,750	4,100
Current assets		
Inventories	320	208
Trade receivables	360	231
Cash and cash equivalents	0	68
	680	507
Total assets	5,430	4,607
Current liabilities		
Trade payables	(195)	(139)
Tax liabilities	(44)	(22)
Bank overdraft	(152)	0
	(391)	(161)
Net current assets	289	346
Non-current liabilities		
Bank loans	(1,300)	(800)
Total liabilities	(1,691)	(961)
Net assets	3,739	3,646
Equity		
Share capital	2,500	2,500
Retained earnings	1,239	1,146
Total equity	3,739	3,646

Task 2.1

Prepare a report for Sally Forth that includes the following:

a) the formulae that are used to calculate each of the following ratios:

i) gross profit ratio
ii) net profit ratio
iii) inventories turnover in days (based on cost of sales)
iv) trade receivables turnover in days (trade receivables collection period)

b) a calculation of the above ratios for the two years

c) a comment on the relative performance of the company for the two years based on the ratios calculated and what this tells you about the company

d) ONE suggestion as to how EACH of the ratios might be improved.

Task 2.2

a)   Set out the accounting equation and define the elements in the equation.
b)   Briefly explain how the profit for the year affects the elements in the accounting equation.

ANSWERS

1 i)   Investors in a business will require information that helps them to judge how well the management of the business have performed and allows them to make decisions as to whether to continue to invest in the business.

ii)   Loan creditors will be concerned with the ability of the business to pay the interest on the loan periodically and to repay the loan as it falls due. Therefore loan creditors will be concerned about both the short and the long term stability and liquidity of the business.

iii) Employees will require information that helps them to assess the ability of the business to continue into the future and to pay their wages and other benefits. They will therefore be interested in the stability and profitability of the business.

iv)   In order to run the business efficiently the management of a business will require financial information about the past performance of the business and also about its current position on a regular basis.

2 There are three main differences between a sole trader and a limited company.

i)   A limited company is a separate legal entity distinct from its owners. Therefore a company can enter into contracts, purchase assets and incur liabilities in its own name.

ii)   In a sole trader's business the owner, the sole trader, is normally also the person who runs the business. However in many limited companies the owners are the shareholders but they delegate the running of the business to directors of the company.

iii) The shareholders in a limited company have limited liability for the debts of the company. This means that if the company does not have enough funds to pay its creditors the shareholders are not personally liable to make up the difference. If a company ceases trading the shareholders lose only the capital that they have already invested in the company. In contrast if a sole trader's business is unable to pay its creditors the sole trader will be personally liable for the debts and will be required to meet the liabilities from his own private resources.

3 i) Relevant information is information that has the ability to influence the economic decisions of users.

ii) Reliable information is information that:

- can be depended upon to represent faithfully what it purports to represent or could be reasonably expected to represent

- is free from deliberate bias or material error

- is complete

- in its preparation under conditions of uncertainty, a degree of caution has been applied when exercising judgement.

4

International Accounting Standards Committee Foundation
appoints Trustees, who appoint the members of the other bodies and is responsible for governance, fundraising and public awareness of the IASB.

Standards Advisory Council
advises the IASB during the standard setting process. It consists of groups and individuals from many different countries and backgrounds.

International Accounting Standards Board
develops, issues and withdraws accounting standards. Its members are chosen for their technical expertise, rather than because of their nationality.

International Financial Reporting Interpretations Committee
provides timely guidance on financial reporting issues not covered by IASs/IFRSs and on the application and interpretations of IASs/IFRSs. Issues Interpretations setting out the accounting treatment that should be adopted for specific items.

5   The objectives of the IASB are to:

- develop a single set of high quality global accounting standards to help participants in the world's capital markets and other users make economic decisions;

- promote the use and rigorous application of those standards;

- to take account of, as appropriate, the special needs of small- and medium-sized entities and emerging economies; and

- bring about convergence of national accounting standards and International Accounting Standards.

6   The main purposes of the IASB's Framework for the Preparation and Presentation of Financial Statements are:

- to assist the IASB in its development of future international accounting standards and in the review of existing standards;

- to assist preparers of financial statements in applying international accounting standards and in dealing with topics that do not form the subject of an accounting standard;

- to assist users of financial statements in interpreting the information contained in financial statements which have been prepared in accordance with international accounting standards.

7   The historical cost concept.

8   i)   The accruals or matching concept requires that income and expenses should be accounted for in the period that they are earned or incurred rather than in the period in which the cash is received or paid. This means that at the end of each accounting period the expenses of the business must be considered to determine whether there are any accrued expenses or prepaid expenses.

ii)   The going concern concept is an assumption that is made in the preparation of the financial statements of a business that the business will continue to operate for the foreseeable future. An example of how this affects the balance sheet is that the non-current assets are recorded at their original cost (or valuation) less accumulated depreciation rather than at their realisable value if they had to be sold.

iii)   The consistency concept is that similar items should be treated in the same way within each accounting period and items should be treated in the same way from one accounting period to the next. Therefore once a business has determined its accounting policies for items in the financial statements then these policies should not be changed unless there is good reason to change them.

iv) The prudence concept concerns the exercise of judgement in conditions of uncertainty when preparing financial statements. Prudence means that a cautious approach should be taken when judgements are being made so that assets and gains are not overstated and that liabilities and losses are not understated. The setting up of a provision (allowance) for doubtful debts is an example of the prudence concept in the preparation of the financial statements.

v) The materiality concept is the assumption that accounting standards and other regulations only have to be applied to material items. An item is viewed to be material if its misstatement or omission from the financial statements might reasonably be expected to influence the economic decisions of users of the financial statements. An example of materiality in practice is where small, immaterial non-current assets, such as calculators in an accounts department, would be written off as an expense in the income statement rather than being included in the balance sheet with other non-current assets.

vi) The money measurement concept is that only items that can be measured reliably at a monetary amount should be included in the financial statements. This means that assets such as the technical expertise of the workforce cannot be included as an asset.

9   i) An asset is a resource controlled by the entity as a result of past events and from which future economic benefits are expected to flow to the entity.

ii) A liability is a present obligation of an entity arising from past events, the settlement of which is expected to result in an outflow from the entity of resources embodying economic benefits.

iii) Income is increases in economic benefits during the accounting period in the form of increases of assets or decreases of liabilities that result in increases of equity, other than those relating to contributions from owners.

iv) Expenses are decreases in economic benefits during the accounting period in the form of decreases of assets or increases in liabilities that result in decreases in equity, other than those relating to distributions to owners.

10 i) Assets – liabilities   = Equity

ii) Equity   = Contributions from owners + income – expenses
       – distributions from owners

11 i) Suppliers may be interested in the financial statements in order to decide whether to carry on supplying goods on credit (by looking at the liquidity position).

ii) Potential investors may need this information to decide whether or not they should invest in the company.

iii) The bank may wish to decide whether to continue an overdraft facility or grant a loan by assessing profitability and liquidity.

answers to chapter 2: INTRODUCTION TO LIMITED COMPANIES

1   i)   Separate legal personality means that a limited company is a separate entity from the owners from a legal viewpoint. It can enter into contracts, acquire assets and incur liabilities in its own name.

    ii) Limited liability means that the shareholders liability is limited to the amount that they have paid for their shares. This means that if the company becomes insolvent the maximum that the shareholders can lose is the amount that they have invested in the company's shares.

    iii) Ordinary shares are also known as equity shares. Ordinary shares entitle the holder to a share in the profits of the company after all prior claims such as debenture interest and preference dividends. The amount of profits paid out to the holders of the ordinary shares, the dividend, is declared by the directors of the company. The holders of ordinary shares can vote in general meetings and therefore are the effective owners of the company.

    iv) Preference shares are shares which carry the right to a fixed rate of dividend. The preference dividend must be paid out of available profits before any ordinary dividend is paid and the holders of the preference shares do not have a right to vote in general meetings.

    v)   The directors of a company are appointed by the ordinary shareholders to manage the company on the shareholders' behalf. In many small companies the directors and the shareholders are the same people but in larger companies although the directors may own some ordinary shares they will be managing the company on behalf of the majority of external shareholders.

2   There are a number of advantages to trading as a limited company.

    ■   The limited liability of the owners of the company

    ■   Limited companies have a wider market for raising finance, for example rights issues and debenture loans

    ■   A company continues to operate even if the shareholdings change hands

    ■   The investors in a company can easily disinvest by simply selling their shares

    ■   Limited companies pay corporation tax rather than the individual shareholders paying tax on the company profits.

There are also some disadvantages to operating as a limited company.

- Limited companies must publish their annual accounts

- The annual accounts of most limited companies must be audited

- Limited companies must comply with many legal and accounting regulations

- When issuing shares limited companies must comply with the requirements of the Companies Act and it may be difficult to reduce the share capital if this is found to be necessary.

3

	Distributable	Non-distributable
Revaluation reserve		X
Retained earnings reserve	X	
Share premium account		X
Plant replacement reserve	X	
General reserve	X	

4 Debentures are a long-term loan to a company. They carry a fixed rate of interest.

The differences between debentures and share capital are:

- debenture holders are creditors of the company whilst ordinary shareholders are the owners of the company

- debenture holders receive a fixed rate of interest on their investment whereas the ordinary dividend will fluctuate as it is declared by the directors

- debenture interest is an expense of the company in the income statement whereas the ordinary dividend is a distribution to owners

- the debenture interest must be paid otherwise the debenture holders can take legal action against the company whereas there is no requirement for the directors of a company to declare an ordinary dividend

- debentures normally have a fixed repayment date but ordinary share capital will normally only be repaid when the company is wound up

- debenture holders cannot vote in general meeting unlike the ordinary shareholders

- debentures may be secured on various assets of the company whereas ordinary shares are unsecured.

5 i) 1 January 20X0 – issue of shares

		£	£
Debit	Bank (100,000 x £0.80)	80,000	
Credit	Share capital (100,000 x £0.50)		50,000
Credit	Share premium (100,000 x £0.30)		30,000

ii) 1 January 20X1 – bonus issue

		£	£
Debit	Share premium account	10,000	
Credit	Share capital account		10,000

iii) 31 December 20X1 – rights issue

		£	£
Debit	Bank (30,000 x £1.00)	30,000	
Credit	Share capital (30,000 x £0.50)		15,000
Credit	Share premium (30,000 x £0.50)		15,000

6 **Income statement for the year ended 31 March 20X2**

	£	£
Revenue		940,000
Cost of sales (47,000 + 564,000 – 52,000)		(559,000)
Gross profit		381,000
Distribution costs	100,000	
Administrative expenses	96,000	
		(196,000)
Profit from operations		185,000
Finance costs (50,000 x 8%)		(4,000)
Profit before tax		181,000
Tax		(48,000)
Profit for the year		133,000

Balance sheet as at 31 March 20X2

	£	£
Non-current assets		
Property, plant and equipment		
Land and buildings (400,000 – 80,000)		320,000
Plant (100,000 – 60,000)		40,000
Office equipment (20,000 – 10,000)		10,000
		370,000
Current assets		
Inventories	52,000	
Trade and other receivables (156,000 + 7,000)	163,000	
Cash (1,700 + 200)	1,900	
		216,900
		586,900
Current liabilities		
Trade and other payables	141,000	
Accruals (12,000 + 2,000)	14,000	
Tax liabilities	48,000	
	203,000	
Non-current liabilities		
8% Debenture	50,000	
Total liabilities		253,000
Net assets		333,900
Equity		
Share capital		100,000
Share premium		50,000
Retained earnings (52,500 + 133,000 – 1,600)		183,900
		333,900

1   According to both IAS 1 *Presentation of financial statements* and the IASB Framework, the objective of financial statements is to provide information about the financial position, financial performance and cash flows of an entity that is useful to a wide range of users in making economic decisions.

Financial statements also show the results of management's stewardship of the resources entrusted to it.

2   There is no definition of 'true and fair view' or fair presentation in either the Companies Act or accounting standards. However, IAS 1 states that fair presentation requires the faithful presentation of the effects of transactions, other events and conditions in accordance with the definitions and recognition criteria for assets, liabilities, income and expenses set out in the IASB's Framework.

It is generally recognised that financial statements will give a fair presentation if they comply with applicable accounting standards (IASs and IFRSs).

3   Financial statements must be prepared on a going concern basis, unless the entity is not a going concern.

4 **Income statement for the year ended ....**

	£'000	£'000
Continuing operations		
Revenue		X
Cost of sales		X
Gross profit		X
Other operating income		X
Distribution costs		X
Administrative expenses		X
Profit from operations		X
Finance costs		X
Profit before tax		X
Tax		X
Profit for the period from continuing operations		X
Discontinued operations		
Loss for the period from discontinued operations		X
Profit for the period attributable to equity holders		X

5
- Trade and other payables
- Tax liabilities
- Bank loans and overdrafts

6 Any six of the following:

- Fair review of the business for the year and the position at the end of the year

- Principal activities of the business for the year and any significant changes

- Estimates of any significant differences between the book value and market value of fixed assets

- Amount of any proposed dividend

- Names of directors during the year

- Interests of each director in shares or debentures of the company at the start of the year and at the end of the year

- Political and charitable donations if they exceed more than £200 in total

- Any significant post balance sheet events

- Indication of likely future developments of the business

- Indication of the research and development activities

- Details of purchase of its own shares by the company

- Company policy for employment of disabled persons (if number of employees is more than 250)

- Company policy regarding employee involvement (if number of employees is more than 250)

- Payment policy towards creditors (if a plc or large private company).

7 A **discontinued operation** is a component of an entity that has either been disposed of or is **held for sale** and represents a separate **major line of business** or **geographical area** of operations.

8 **Diverge Ltd**
Income statement for the year ended 31 December 20X3

	£'000
Continuing operations	
Revenue (12,134 – 364)	11,770
Cost of sales (5,451 – 236)	(5,215)
Gross profit	6,555
Distribution costs (1,758 – 70)	(1,688)
Administrative expenses (1,041 – 53)	(988)
Profit from operations (3,884 – 5)	3,879
Finance costs (305 – 142)	(163)
Profit before tax	3,716
Tax	(1,144)
Profit for the period from continuing operations	2,572
Discontinued operations	
Loss for the period from discontinued operations (142 – 5)	(137)
Profit for the year attributable to equity holders	2,435

9 **Paparazzi Ltd**
Income statement for the year ended 30 June 20X2

	£'000
Continuing operations	
Revenue (15,200 – 500)	14,700
Cost of sales (690 + 10,960 – 180 – 710)	(10,760)
Gross profit	3,940
Distribution costs	(1,200)
Administrative expenses	(2,120)
Profit from operations	620
Finance costs	(84)
Profit before tax	536
Tax	(130)
Profit for the year from continuing operations attributable to equity holders	406

Paparazzi Ltd
Balance sheet as at 30 June 20X2

	£'000
Non-current assets: property, plant and equipment (W1)	3,272
Current assets:	
Inventories	710
Trade and other receivables (W2)	2,448
Cash and cash equivalents	567
	3,725
Total assets	6,997
Current liabilities:	
Trade and other payables (1,400 + 50)	1,450
Tax liabilities	130
	1,580
Net current assets	2,145
Non-current liabilities:	
Loan stock	1,200
Total liabilities	2,780
Net assets	4,217
Equity:	
Share capital	2,500
Share premium	300
Retained earnings (W3)	1,417
	4,217

Workings

1 *Property, plant and equipment*

	Cost	Acc depn	NBV
	£'000	£'000	£'000
Land and buildings	2,100	280	1,820
Plant and machinery	1,050	194	856
Fixtures and fittings	380	128	252
Motor vehicles	620	276	344
	4,150	878	3,272

2 *Trade and other receivables*

	£'000
Trade receivables	2,500
Less provision for doubtful debts	(92)
	2,408
Prepayments	40
	2,448

3   *Retained earnings*

	£'000
Per TB	1,131
Profit for year	406
Dividends paid	(120)
	1,417

10 a)   The journal entries required are as follows.

	Debit £'000	Credit £'000
Corporation tax (income statement)	972	
Corporation tax (payables)		972
Interest charge (income statement) (8% x £3,600,000 x 1/12)	24	
Accruals		24

b)   FUN LIMITED
      INCOME STATEMENT FOR THE YEAR ENDED 31 SEPTEMBER 20X8

Continuing operations	£'000
Revenue (W1)	14,363
Cost of sales (W2)	6,464
Gross profit	7,899
Distribution costs	2,669
Administrative expenses	2,042
Profit from operations	3,188
Finance costs (300+24)	324
Profit before tax	2,864
Tax	972
Profit for the year for continuing operations attributable to equity holders	1,892

Workings

1   *Revenue*

	£'000
Sales	14,595
Returns inwards	(232)
	14,363

2   *Cost of sales*

	£'000
Opening inventories	1,893
Purchases	6,671
Carriage inwards	87
Returns outwards	(146)
Closing inventories	(2,041)
	6,464

c)   NOTES FOR BOARD MEETING DEALING WITH ACCOUNTING MATTERS

i)   A share premium arises when a company sells shares for a price which is higher than the nominal value. By 'premium' is meant the difference between the issue price of the share and its nominal value. For example, if a share with a nominal value of £1 was issued for £1.20, then the accounting entries would be:

DEBIT	Cash	£1.20	
CREDIT	Share capital		£1.00
CREDIT	Share premium		£0.20

The revaluation reserve arose because at some point a non-current asset was revalued. The balance represents the excess of the fair value of the asset over its net value. For example, if the asset had a net book value of £600,000, and its market value was £950,000, the accounting entries would be:

DEBIT	Property, plant and equipment	£350,000	
CREDIT	Revaluation reserve		£350,000

ii)   It is by no means certain that a leased asset can be kept off the balance sheet. The accounting treatment of leased assets is governed by IAS 17 Leases.

The correct treatment depends on whether the lease is a finance lease or an operating lease. IAS 17 defines a finance lease as a lease which transfers substantially all the risks and rewards of ownership of an asset to the lessee. An operating lease is a lease other than a finance lease.

If the lease is a finance lease, it should be recorded in Fun Ltd's balance sheet as an asset and as an obligation to pay future rentals. The amount recorded should be the present value of the minimum lease payments derived by discounting them at the interest rate implicit in the lease.

If, however, the lease is an operating lease, the asset belongs to the lessor, and so is not shown on the balance sheet of Fun Ltd. Rentals are charged to the income statement, but future rentals are not shown as a liability on the balance sheet of Fun Ltd.

11

					£	£
a)	i)	DEBIT	Taxation charge		110,000	
		CREDIT	Taxation payable			110,000
	ii)	DEBIT	Motor expenses		10,000	
		DEBIT	Wages		2,000	
		CREDIT	General expenses			12,000
	iii)	DEBIT	Loan interest (income statement)		2,000	
		CREDIT	Interest payable			2,000
	iv)	DEBIT	Audit fees (income statement)		9,000	
		CREDIT	Accruals			9,000
	v)	No adjustment is needed				

vi)   No adjustment is needed

vii) No adjustment is needed

viii) No adjustment is needed

ix)   No adjustment is needed

b)   FRANCO LIMITED
     INCOME STATEMENT FOR THE YEAR ENDED 31 MARCH 20X5

	£'000
Continuing operations	
Revenue	2,460
Cost of sales	999
Gross profit	1,461
Distribution costs	416
Administrative expenses	341
Profit from operations	704
Finance cost	2
Profit before tax	702
Tax	110
Profit for the year for continuing operations attributable to equity holders	592

FRANCO LIMITED
BALANCE SHEET AS AT MARCH 20X5

	£'000
Non-current assets	
Property, plant and equipment	608
Current assets	
Inventories	225
Receivables	447
Cash and cash equivalents	7
	679
Total assets	1,287
Current liabilities	
Trade payables	170
Tax liabilities	110
Accruals (4 + 9)	13
Interest payable	2
	295
Net current assets	384
Non-current liabilities	
Long term loan	20
Total liabilities	315
Net assets	972
Equity	
Share capital	250
Retained earnings	722
	972

Workings

1   Revenue

	£'000
Per ETB	2,470
Less returns inwards	(10)
	2,460

2   Cost of sales

Opening inventories	215
Purchases	1,000
Plus carriage inwards	14
Less: returns outwards	(5)
	1,224
Less: closing inventories	(225)
	999

3   Distribution costs and administrative expenses

		Administrative expenses £	Distribution costs £
Depreciation:	buildings	3,000	1,000
	fixtures and fittings	4,000	1,000
	motor vehicles	2,000	8,000
	office	1,000	–
Insurance (75/25)		9,000	3,000
Rates		10,000	10,000
Light and heat		18,000	18,000
Audit		9,000	–
Advertising		–	95,000
Increase in provision for doubtful debts		3,000	–
General expenses (135 – 12)		100,000	23,000
Motor expenses (27 + 10)		10,000	27,000
Directors' emoluments		68,000	30,000
Salaries and wages (400 – 98 + 2)		104,000	200,000
		341,000	416,000

4   Receivables

	£'000
Trade receivables	450
Less: provision for doubtful debts	(9)
	441
Prepayments	6
	447

5 *Property, plant and equipment*

	Cost £'000	Accum depn £'000	Net book value £'000
Land and buildings	575	24	551
Fixtures and fittings	35	23	12
Motor vehicles	94	64	30
Office equipment	20	5	15
	724	116	608

6 *Retained earnings*

	£'000
As at 1 April 20X4	160
Profit for the year	592
Dividends paid	(30)
As at 31 March 20X5	722

c) REPORT

To: The Directors
Franco Ltd

From: Accounting Technician   Date: 5 April 20X5

Inventory valuation

IAS 2 states that inventories must be valued at the lower of cost and net realisable value.

Cost is all costs of purchase, costs of conversion and other costs incurred in bringing the inventories to their present location and condition. This expenditure should include:

i) Costs of purchase: purchase price, import duties, other taxes, transport and handling costs and any other directly attributable costs, less trade discounts, rebates and subsidies.

ii) Costs of conversion: costs directly related to the units of production, such as direct labour. They also include fixed and variable production overheads

Net realisable value is the estimated selling price in the ordinary course of business less:

i) the estimated costs of completion
ii) the estimated costs necessary to make the sale

Comparison of cost and net realisable value should be made for each item or category of inventory separately rather than comparing total cost with total NRV.

12 a) | | | £'000 | £'000 |

i) No adjustment needed

ii) No adjustment needed

iii) No adjustment needed

iv) DEBIT Tax charge (I/S) 211
CREDIT Corporation tax payable 211

v) DEBIT Interest payable (I/S) 15
CREDIT Accruals (300 x 10% x 6/12) 15

vi) DEBIT Distribution costs 19
CREDIT Accruals 19

vii) DEBIT Administrative expenses 8
CREDIT Investments (64 − 56) 8

b) DOWANGO LIMITED
INCOME STATEMENT FOR THE YEAR ENDED 31 MARCH 20X6

£'000

Continuing operations

	£'000
Revenue (W1)	5,352
Cost of sales (W2)	2,910
Gross profit	2,442
Distribution costs (1,104 + 19)	1,123
Administrative expenses (709 + 8)	717
Profit from operations	602
Finance costs (15 + 15)	30
Profit before tax	572
Tax	211
Profit for the year from continuing operations attributable to equity holders	361

DOWANGO LIMITED
BALANCE SHEET AS AT 31 MARCH 20X6

	£'000
Non-current assets	
Property, plant and equipment (W3)	1,153
Current assets	
Investment	56
Inventories	365
Receivables (W4)	613
Cash and cash equivalents	3
	1,037
Total assets	2,190
Current liabilities	
Trade payables	331
Tax liabilities	211
Bank overdraft	157
Accruals (41 + 15 + 19)	75
	774
Net current assets	263
Non-current liabilities	300
Total liabilities	1,074
Net assets	1,116
Equity	
Share capital	500
Retained earnings (275 + 361 - 20)	616
	1,116

Workings

1   *Revenue*

	£'000
Sales	5,391
Less returns inwards	(39)
	5,352

2   *Cost of sales*

	£'000
Opening inventories	298
Purchases	2,988
Carriage inwards	20
Less: returns outwards	(31)
	3,275
Less: closing inventories	(365)
	2,910

3   Property, plant and equipment

	Cost £'000	Acc. depn. £'000	NBV £'000
Land	431	–	431
Buildings	512	184	328
Fixtures and fittings	389	181	208
Motor vehicles	341	204	137
Office equipment	105	56	49
	1,778	625	1,153

4   Receivables

	£'000
Trade receivables	619
Less provision	(27)
	592
Prepayments	21
	613

13   a)   The journal entries required are as follows.

	Debit £'000	Credit £'000
Tax charge (income statement)	75	
Tax payable		75
Interest charge (income statement) (10% x £200,000 x 6/12)	10	
Accruals		10
Bad debt expense (W)	9	
Provision for bad debts		9

Working: Bad debt expense

Receivables per ETB	£500,000
Provision required (£500,000 x 2%)	£10,000
Increase in provision (10 – 1)	£9,000

b)   SOLU LIMITED
INCOME STATEMENT FOR THE YEAR ENDED 31 MARCH 20X8

Continuing operations	£'000
Revenue	4,090
Cost of sales (W1)	1,805
Gross profit	2,285
Distribution costs	1,055
Administrative expenses (W2)	999
Profit from operations	231
Finance costs (W3)	20
Profit before tax	211
Tax	75
Profit for the year for continuing operations attributable to equity holders	136

Workings

1   *Cost of sales*

	£'000
Opening inventories	300
Purchases	1,800
Carriage inwards	25
Closing inventories	(320)
	1,805

2   *Administrative expenses*

	£'000
Per ETB	990
Increase in bad debt prov'n	9
	999

3   *Finance costs*

	£'000
Per ETB	10
Accrual	10
	20

14   **Tutorial note**: In Part c) your answer should be in terms of IAS 37 *Provisions, contingent liabilities and contingent assets*.

a)   The journal entries required are as follows.

	Debit £'000	Credit £'000
Tax charge (income statement)	11.0	
Tax payable		11.0
Interest charge (income statement) (12% x £100,000 x 1/12)	1.0	
Accruals		1.0
Bad debt expense	10.0	
Receivables		10.0
Bad debt expense (W)	5.8	
Provision for bad debts		5.8

Working

Increase in bad debt provision

	£'000
Trade receivables per ETB	370
Less bad debt written off	(10)
Adjusted trade receivables at 30.9.X8	360
Provision required (3% x 360)	10.8
Existing provision	(5.0)
Increase in provision	5.8

b) BATHLEA LIMITED
INCOME STATEMENT FOR THE YEAR ENDED 31 SEPTEMBER 20X8

Continuing operations	£'000
Revenue	3,509.0
Cost of sales (W1)	1,641.0
Gross profit	1868.0
Distribution costs	857.0
Administrative expenses (W2)	907.8
Profit from operations	103.2
Finance cost (11+1)	12.0
Profit before tax	91.2
Tax	11.0
Profit for the year for continuing operations attributable to equity holders	80.2

BATHLEA LIMITED
BALANCE SHEET AS AT 31 SEPTEMBER 20X8

	£'000
Non-current assets	
Property, plant and equipment (W3)	500.0
Current assets	
Inventories	250.0
Receivables (W4)	359.2
	609.2
Total assets	1,109.2
Current liabilities	
Trade and other payables	350.0
Tax liabilities	11.0
Bank overdraft	3.0
Accruals (9 + 1)	10.0
	374.0
Net current assets	235.2
Non-current liabilities	100.0
Total liabilities	474.0
Net assets	635.2
Equity	
Share capital	500.0
Retained earnings (W6)	135.2
	635.2

Workings

1   *Cost of sales*

	£'000
Opening inventories	200
Purchases	1,600
Carriage inwards	91
Closing inventories	(250)
	1,641

2   *Administrative expenses*

	£'000
Per ETB	892.0
Bad debt written off	10.0
Increase in bad debt provision	5.8
	907.8

3   *Property, plant and equipment*

	Cost	Acc. depn.	NBV
	£'000	£'000	£'000
Land and buildings	300	65	235
Fixtures and fittings	220	43	177
Motor vehicles	70	27	43
Office equipment	80	35	45
	670	170	500

4   *Receivables*

	£'000
Per ETB	370.0
Bad debt written off	(10.0)
Bad debt provision	(10.8)
Prepayment	10.0
	359.2

5   *Retained earnings*

	£'000
Retained earnings b/f	70.0
Profit for the year	80.2
Dividend paid	(15.0)
Retained earnings c/f	135.2

c)   The law suit is a contingent liability and, as such is governed by IAS 37 *Provisions, contingent liabilities and contingent assets*. IAS 37 defines a contingent liability as:

'A possible obligation that arises from past events and whose existence will be confirmed only by the occurrence or non-occurrence of one or more uncertain future events not wholly within the entity's control'.

Under IAS 37, a contingent liability should never be accrued for in the accounts – if the outflow is probable, the item is a provision. If the outflow is merely possible, a contingent liability should be disclosed. However, in this case the possibility of an outflow is remote so there is no need to disclose or provide.

1 Net profit attributable to ordinary shareholders = £170,000

Number of shares = 1,000,000 x 4/12 + 1,400,000 x 8/12
= 333,333 + 933,333
= 1,266,666

EPS $= \dfrac{£170,000}{1,266,666}$

= 13.4 pence

2 Accounting policies are defined in IAS 8 as the 'specific principles, bases, conventions, rules and practices applied by an entity in preparing and presenting financial statements'.

Therefore an accounting policy will determine how and when an item is recognised, the basis on which the item is measured and how the item is presented.

Accounting estimates are made in order to arrive at amounts such as the useful lives of assets. There are accepted methods of making accounting estimates.

An example of an accounting policy is that property, plant and equipment are depreciated over their useful lives. The method of depreciation used, straight line or reducing balance, is an example of an accounting estimate.

3 False. An accounting policy can also be changed where a new policy would result in the financial statements providing reliable and more relevant information.

4

	20X2 £	20X1 £
Retained earnings at the beginning of the year:		
As previously reported	140,000	60,000
Change in accounting policy	(24,000)	(12,000)
Restated	116,000	48,000
Retained earnings for the year	90,000	68,000
Retained earnings at the end of the year	206,000	116,000

5   Income statement

	£
Profit before tax	150,000
Tax	(40,000)
Profit for the year	110,000

Statement of recognised income and expense

	£
Gain on revaluation of property, plant and equipment	70,000
Profit for the year	110,000
Total recognised income and expense for the year	180,000

Total movements in equity

	£
Balance at 1 May 20X1	810,000
Gain in property revaluations	70,000
Profit for the year	110,000
Dividends (700,000 x 5p)	(35,000)
New share capital (200,000 x 1.40)	280,000
Balance at 30 April 20X2	1,235,000

6   IFRS 8 applies to public companies. It states that an entity should disclose the following information for each of its operating segments:

- profit or loss
- total assets
- total liabilities (if management uses this information to make decisions about the entity).

Entities must also disclose:

- the factors used to identify the entity's reportable segments, including the basis of segmentation (for example, whether segments are based on products and services, geographical areas or a combination of these)

- the types of products and services from which each reportable segment derives its revenues.

7   This is a material prior period error. IAS 8 states that the financial statements should be corrected to restate the financial statements as if the error had never occurred.

This means that in the financial statements for the year ended 31 December 20X4, the opening balance of retained earnings is adjusted and the comparative figures for 20X3 are restated. The adjustment is separately disclosed in the statement of changes in equity or adjacent to the statement of recognised income and expense.

1 The profit reported in a company's income statement will never be the same as the increase in cash in a company's balance sheet over the same period. Indeed even if large profits have been made a company may see a fall in the amount of cash held or an increase in the bank overdraft.

The profit recorded in the income statement is determined using the accruals or matching concept. This means that income and expenses are recognised in the income statement in the period in which they were incurred and not necessarily in the period in which the cash was paid or received.

The figures that appear in the income statement and balance sheet are often subjective and may depend upon the accounting policies and estimates used by the company and the judgement of the directors when making estimates such as the expected useful life of property, plant and equipment. Cash flow however is a matter of fact which cannot be distorted by policies or judgements.

The income statement will include non-cash expenses such as depreciation and profits or losses on sales of non-current assets and therefore will not equate directly to cash flow.

Finally any profits made will be put to many uses such as increasing non-current assets or investing further in working capital. Only the residual figure will cause any increase or decrease in cash balances.

2 **Indirect method**

	£
Profit from operations (100,000 + 10,000)	110,000
Depreciation	20,000
Increase in inventories (30,000 – 25,000)	(5,000)
Decrease in receivables (40,000 – 42,000)	2,000
Decrease in payables (28,000 – 32,000)	(4,000)
Cash generated from operations	123,000
Interest paid	(10,000)
Tax paid	(25,000)
Net cash from operating activities	88,000

3 i)

Interest paid

	£		£
Cash paid (bal fig)	37,400	Balance b/d	13,000
Balance c/d	8,000	Income statement	32,400
	45,400		45,400

ii)

Tax paid

	£		£
Cash paid (bal fig)	92,000	Balance b/d	94,000
Balance c/d	100,000	Income statement	98,000
	192,000		192,000

4 i)

Property, plant and equipment at cost

	£000		£000
Balance b/d	1,250	Disposals	140
Cash paid (bal fig)	230	Balance c/d	1,340
	1,480		1,480

ii)

	£'000
Net book value	98
Loss on disposal	(23)
Proceeds from sale	75

iii)

Accumulated depreciation

	£000		£000
Disposals (140 – 98)	42	Balance b/d	480
Balance c/d	560	Income statement (bal fig)	122
	602		602

Property, plant and equipment at net book value

	£		£
Balance b/d	830,000	Disposals (60 – (35 – 6))	31,000
		Income statement	120,000
Cash paid (bal fig)	211,000	Balance c/d	890,000
	1,041,000		1,041,000

Cash flow statement for the year ended 30 April 20X2

	£'000
Profit from operations	165
Adjustments for:	
Depreciation (W1)	93
	258
Increase in trade receivables (85 – 77)	(8)
Increase in inventories (110 – 94)	(16)
Increase in trade payables (68 – 43)	25
Cash generated from operations	259
Interest paid	(17)
Income taxes paid (W2)	(30)
Net cash from operating activities	212

Cash flows from investing activities		
Purchase of property, plant and equipment (W3)	(247)	
Proceeds from sale of non-current asset (26 – 9)	17	
Dividends received	8	
Net cash used in investing activities		(222)
Cash flows from financing activities		
Proceeds from issue of share capital (60 – 50 + 25 – 20)	15	
Proceeds from long term loan (180 – 130)	50	
Dividends paid (W4)	(45)	
Net cash from financing activities		20
Net increase in cash and cash equivalents		10
Cash and cash equivalents at 1 April 20X1 (Note)		41
Cash and cash equivalents at 31March 20X2 (Note)		51

Note: Cash and cash equivalents

	At 1 April 20X1 £'000	Cash flows £'000	At 31 March 20X2 £'000
Cash	24	(24)	–
Bank overdraft	–	(17)	(17)
	24	(41)	(17)
Investments	17	51	68
	41	10	51

Workings

Working 1

Property, plant and equipment – accumulated depreciation

	£000		£000
Disposals (43 – 26)	17	Balance b/d	128
Balance c/d	204	Income statement (bal fig)	93
	221		221

Working 2

Taxation

	£000		£000
Cash paid (bal fig)	30	Balance b/d	34
Balance c/d	42	Income statement	38
	72		72

Working 3

Property, plant and equipment at cost

	£000		£000
Balance b/d	408	Disposals	43
Cash paid (bal fig)	247	Balance c/d	612
	655		655

Working 4

Retained earnings (dividends)

	£000		£000
Cash paid (bal fig)	45	Balance b/d	215
Balance c/d	279	Profit for the year	109
	324		324

7 Cash and cash equivalents

	£'000
Cash and cash equivalents at 1 July 20X1 (8,000 + 3,000)	11,000
Cash and cash equivalents at 30 June 20X2 (14,000 + 1,000 - 12,000)	(3,000)
Decrease in cash and cash equivalents	(8,000)

8 There are many advantages to published cash flow statements including the following.

- They allow users to assess any possible liquidity problems of the company

- They show the company's ability to turn profit into cash

- Cash flow is a matter of fact and it cannot be affected by accounting policies or judgemental decisions

- The cash flow statement may help users predict the future cash flows of the company and its financial adaptability

- Cash flow is easier to understand than profit

- The standard format of the published cash flow statement means that users can compare different companies.

There are also some limitations in the use of cash flow statements.

- The cash flow statement is based upon year end balance sheet balances which can be manipulated

- The cash flow statement is based upon historical cost data and therefore may not necessarily be a useful indicator of future cash flows

- A cash flow statement concentrates on the cash position but in the longer term a company must have profits if it is to survive. This often means that a company must sacrifice cash flow in the shorter term, for example by using cash to invest in property, plant and equipment.

9   The first element of the cash flow statement to be noted is that the net cash from operating activities is about 25% higher than the operating profit indicating the company's ability to convert profit from operations into cash flows.

However the significant cash inflow from operating profit has been used up, with a total decrease in cash of £189,000. By far the most significant use of the cash is in the purchase of property, plant and equipment. This, together with the interest, tax and dividend payments, has used up all of the cash flow from operations. However the decrease in cash has been offset to some extent by a substantial issue of loan stock during the year.

It would appear that the strategy of the management is that of substantial growth in operating capacity given the investment in non-current assets. There is also a significant increase in both inventory and receivables, not matched by an increase in payables however, which also indicates a growth strategy.

Despite the decrease in cash this year the signs are that the company is able to produce cash from its operating activities and once the new investments in non-current assets and inventories reach fruition this could lead to a stronger position for the company. Clearly the company has chosen to partly fund this growth by issuing loan stock. Without the details of the income statement and the balance sheet however it is difficult to conclude much more.

10 PATON LIMITED
RECONCILIATION OF PROFIT FROM OPERATIONS
TO NET CASH FROM OPERATING ACTIVITIES
FOR THE YEAR ENDED 30 SEPTEMBER 20X1

	£'000
Profit from operations	5,938
Add: depreciation charge	2,007
Less: profit on sale of non-current asset	(131)
Increase in inventories (7,420 – 6,823)	(597)
Increase in receivables (4,122 – 3,902)	(220)
Increase in payables (1,855 – 1,432)	423
Cash generated from operations	7,420
Interest paid	(392)
Income taxes paid	(1,327)
Net cash from operating activities	5,701

11 i) EVANS

CASH FLOW STATEMENT FOR THE YEAR ENDED 31 OCTOBER 20X1

	£'000	£'000	£'000
Cash flows from operating activities			
Profit from operations		431	
Adjustments for			
Depreciation			
Vehicles (W)	120		
Furniture (270 – 200)	70		
		190	
		621	
Operating profit before working capital changes			
Decrease in inventory (505 – 486)		19	
Increase in receivables (790 – 577)		(213)	
Increase in payables (560 – 546)		14	
		441	
Cash generated from operations			
Interest paid		(35)	
Income taxes paid		(106)	
Net cash from operating activities			300
Cash flows from investing activities			
Purchase of non-current assets (W)		(425)	
Proceeds of sale of non-current assets		75	
Purchase of investments (155 – 80)		(75)	
Investment income		12	
Net cash used in investing activities			(413)
Cash flows from financing activities			
Proceeds from issuance of share capital			
(1,200 – 1,000) + (315 – 270)		245	
Repayment of loan notes (150 – 50)		(100)	
Dividends paid		(40)	
Net cash from financing activities			105
Net decrease in cash and cash equivalents			(8)
Cash and cash equivalents at 1 November 20X0			10
Cash and cash equivalents at 31 October 20X1			2

Working

Non-current assets and depreciation

VEHICLES: COST

	£'000		£'000
Balance b/f	820	Disposals	155
Additions (bal fig)	225	Balance c/f	890
	1,045		1,045

VEHICLES: ACCUMULATED DEPRECIATION

	£'000		£'000
Disposals (155 – 65)	90	Balance b/f	310
Balance c/f	340	Income statement charge	
		(bal fig)	120
	430		430

VEHICLES: DISPOSALS

	£'000		£'000
Non-current assets	155	Accumulated depn	90
Gain on disposal	10	Sale proceeds (bal fig)	75
	165		165

Additions to non-current assets:

	£'000
Vehicles	225
Furniture (900 – 700)	200
	425

ii) While the income statement and balance sheet provide useful information to outside users, it could be argued that the profit figure in the accounts does not always give a meaningful picture of the company's operations. A company's performance and prospects depend not so much on the 'profits' earned in the period, but, more realistically on liquidity or cash flows.

Cash flow statements have the following advantages.

a) They are easier to understand than profit statements.

b) They draw attention to cash flow which is crucial to a business's survival.

c) Suppliers and loan creditors are more interested in a company's ability to pay amounts due than in profitability.

d) Profit depends on accounting conventions and concepts and is thus easy to manipulate.

e) Management decision making is based on future cash flows.

f) Cash flow is easier to audit than profit.

The main disadvantage of a cash flow statement is the reason accruals accounting is used, namely proper matching of related items. In addition, cash flow statements only show the balance at the beginning and end of the year, not how much cash has fluctuated during the year.

12 i) DAWSON
    CASH FLOW STATEMENT FOR THE YEAR ENDED 31 MAY 20X1
    Cash flows from operating activities

	£'000	£'000
Profit from operations (310 + 24)	334	
Adjustments for:		
Depreciation	305	
Amortisation of intangible non-current assets		
(460-450)	10	
Profit on disposal of non-current assets	(85)	
Operating profit before working capital changes	564	
Increase in inventories (500 – 450)	(50)	
Increase in receivables (300 – 270)	(30)	
Increase in payables (220 – 200)	20	
Cash generated from operations	504	
Interest paid	(24)	
Income taxes paid (W1)	(115)	
Net cash from operating activities		365
Cash flows from investing activities		
Purchase of tangible non-current assets (W2)	(665)	
Proceeds of sale of tangible non-current assets (W3)	245	
Purchase of investments (240 – 180)	(60)	
		(480)
Cash flows from financing activities		
Proceeds from issuance of share capital		
(1,200–1,000+15)	215	
Increase in loans (150 – 40)	110	
Dividends paid	(110)	
		215
Net increase in cash and cash equivalents		100
Cash and cash equivalents at 1 June 20X0		(50)
Cash and cash equivalents at 31 May 20X1		50

Workings

1   Corporation tax paid

TAXATION

	£'000		£'000
Tax paid (bal fig)	115	Bal b/d 1 June 20X0	120
Bal c/d 31 May 20X1	125	Income statement charge	120
	240		240

2   Payments to acquire tangible non-current assets

NON-CURRENT ASSETS

	£'000		£'000
Bal b/d 1 June 20X0	1,200	Disposals	160
		Depreciation	305
Additions (bal fig)	665	Bal c/d 31 May 20X1	1,400
	1,865		1,865

3   Proceeds from sale of tangible non-current assets

	£'000
Net book value	160
Profit	85
Proceeds	245

ii)   At first sight Dawson's cash flow appears healthy; the company has gone from a £50,000 overdraft to a £50,000 positive bank balance. However, most of this inflow can be accounted for by a long term loan of £110,000. In other words, the company has merely rescheduled its debt from short to long term.

Much of the cash paid has been invested in new non-current assets, costing £665,000. This has been financed partly by the loan, and partly by the issue of new shares. The aim of this investment will be to generate future profits, and to enable the company to operate more efficiently.

The company generated enough cash from operating activities to meet payments of interest, tax and dividends. It also made a large profit on disposal of non-current assets. However, this is a bookkeeping adjustment and suggests that depreciation was under allowed in previous years.

1   i)   The full cost of the car, including the part exchange value, should be capitalised but the road tax should be charged to the income statement as revenue expenditure.

	£
Balance sheet cost	
Invoice value	14,500
Less: road tax	(150)
Add: part-exchange value	3,000
	17,350

   ii) The legal fees are part of the cost of purchasing the building and should be capitalised. However the redecoration costs would normally be charged to the income statement as revenue expenditure unless the redecoration was essential before the building could be used.

	£
Balance sheet cost	
Purchase price	100,000
Legal fees	4,000
	104,000

   iii) The cost of property, plant and equipment is the cost of bringing it into working condition for its intended use. Therefore the cost will include delivery and installation costs and will also include the necessary cost of the retraining of the staff.

	£
Balance sheet cost	
Purchase price	24,000
Delivery costs	1,000
Installation costs	2,000
Training costs	3,500
	30,500

   iv) The repairs are revenue expenditure and should therefore be charged to the income statement. However the new engine has enhanced the performance of the machine and therefore £15,000 should be capitalised and added to the cost of the machine.

2   i)   IAS 16 allows the revaluation of property, plant and equipment but does not require it – revaluation is optional. However where a business does revalue its property, plant and equipment it must revalue all of the assets in that particular class of property, plant and equipment. The valuation to be used is the fair value (normally the market value) of the item.

Where property, plant and equipment is revalued the valuations should be kept up to date. IAS 16 does not require annual revaluations, but does state that they should be carried out with sufficient regularity to ensure that the carrying value of the item is not materially different from its fair value at the balance sheet date.

Revaluation gains should be taken to a revaluation reserve and reported in the Statement of recognised income and expense. Other revaluation losses are recognised in the Statement of recognised income and expense until the carrying amount of the asset reaches depreciated historical cost. Thereafter any additional loss should be charged to the income statement.

ii)

		£	£
DEBIT	Property at cost (200,000 – 160,000)	40,000	
DEBIT	Accumulated depreciation (2 x 4,000)	8,000	
CREDIT	Revaluation reserve		48,000

iii)   Depreciation charge – year ending 31 March 20X3

£200,000 ÷ 38 = £5,263

3   i)   Depreciation is the measure of the cost or revalued amount of the economic benefits of non-current assets that has been consumed during the period.

When non-current assets are purchased their cost is capitalised in the balance sheet instead of being charged to the income statement. The depreciation charge recognises that the non-current assets are being used within the business to earn income. According to the accruals or matching concept some portion of the original cost or revalued amount is included as a cost in the income statement each year in the form of the depreciation charge.

Therefore the purpose of depreciation is to match the cost of the non-current assets to the income that they earn by spreading the cost of an asset over its useful life and charging a portion of that cost to the income statement each period.

ii)

	£
Cost	30,000
Depreciation charge y/e 30 June 20X1 (30,000 x 40%)	(12,000)
NBV at 30 June 20X1	18,000
Depreciation charge y/e 30 June 20X2 (18,000 x 40%)	(7,200)
NBV at 30 June 20X2	10,800

$$\text{Depreciation charge y/e 30 June 20X3} = \frac{£10,800 - 1,800}{3}$$

$$= £3,000$$

iii) Net book value at 1 January 20X2 = £80,000 – (2 x 8,000)

= £64,000

Remaining useful life at 1 January 20X2 = 7 – 2 years

= 5 years

Depreciation charge y/e 31 December 20X2 = $\dfrac{£64,000}{5}$

= £12,800

4

	£
Carrying value at 31 December 20X5	
£460,000 – (2 x £460,000/46 years)	440,000
Disposal proceeds	500,000
Profit on disposal	60,000

5

	Land and buildings £'000	Plant and machinery £'000	Fixtures and fittings £'000	Total £'000
Cost				
At beginning of year	850	525	176	1,551
Additions	100	–	34	134
Revaluations	–	–	–	–
Disposals	–	(45)	(10)	(55)
At end of year	950	480	200	1,630
Depreciation				
At beginning of year	266	173	70	509
Charge for year	19	94	15	128
Revaluation	–	–	–	–
Disposals	–	(17)	(10)	(27)
	285	250	75	610
Net book value				
At end of year	665	230	125	1,020
At beginning of year	584	352	106	1,042

6 IAS 40 defines an **investment property** as property held to earn rentals or for capital appreciation or for both, rather than for:

- use in the production or supply of goods or services or for administrative purposes; or
- sale in the ordinary course of business.

The following are not investment properties:

- property still under construction
- owner-occupied property.

Under IAS 40 investment properties are either:

- included in the balance sheet at cost and depreciated over their useful lives (in the same way as other items of property, plant and equipment); or

- included in the balance sheet at fair value. Gains and losses on revaluation are recognised in the income statement.

The reason why IAS 40 allows the second option is that investment properties are different in nature from other types of property. They are not 'consumed' within the business and therefore historic cost accounting does not always provide relevant information to users of the financial statements. The information that is useful about investment properties is their fair value and changes in fair value.

7   i)   Research is original and planned investigation undertaken with the prospect of gaining new scientific or technical knowledge and understanding.

Development is the application of research findings or other knowledge to a plan or design for the production of new or substantially improved materials, devices, products, processes, systems before the start of commercial production or use.

ii)   Development expenditure is carried forward and recognised as an intangible asset if all of the following can be demonstrated.

- The technical feasibility of completing the intangible asset so that it will be available for use or sale

- An intention to complete the intangible asset and use or sell it

- Ability to use or sell the intangible asset

- How the intangible asset will generate probable future economic benefits

- The availability of adequate technical, financial and other resources to complete the development and to use or sell the intangible asset

- Ability to measure reliably the expenditure attributable to the intangible asset during its development.

Unless all these conditions are met, the expenditure must be charged to the income statement in the period in which it is incurred.

iii)   Development expenditure normally has a finite useful life and it is amortised over that useful life. Amortisation begins when the asset is available for use (eg when commercial production of the product begins) and continues over the period in which the product or process is expected to be sold or used.

8 i) Goodwill is the excess of the value of a business over and above the fair value of its identifiable assets and liabilities. Goodwill cannot be realised separately from the business – the only way that goodwill can be realised is by selling the business.

Other intangible assets do not have a physical substance but unlike goodwill they are identifiable and can be sold separately from the business without disrupting the business.

ii) IAS 38 states that internally generated goodwill should never be recognised.

9 An impairment review is concerned with a comparison of the carrying amount of an asset in the balance sheet to its recoverable amount. If the recoverable amount is less than the carrying value then an impairment has occurred. Recoverable amount is the higher of the asset's fair value less costs to sell and value in use.

IAS 36 *Impairment of assets* requires that assets should be reviewed for impairment if there is some indication that impairment has occurred.

Impairment losses are recognised in the income statement if the asset has not previously been revalued. If the asset has been previously revalued then the impairment is recognised in the Statement of recognised income and expense down to a carrying value of depreciated historical cost and thereafter in the income statement.

10 NOTES TO THE DIRECTORS

i) *Land at valuation*

IAS 16 *Property, plant and equipment* permits non-current assets to be shown at valuation rather than cost. The increase is calculated as follows.

	£'000
NBV per ETB (268 – 50)	218
Valuation	550
Increase in value	332

The entries required to adjust the accounts are as follows.

DEBIT	Land and buildings	£332,000
CREDIT	Revaluation reserve	£332,000

Depreciation must be charged on the revalued amount.

ii) *Accruals concept*

Revenue and costs are accrued. This means that they are recognised as they are earned or incurred, not as money is received or paid. They are matched with one another and dealt with in the income statement of the period to which they relate.

An example which illustrates the accruals concept is the accrual of interest on a long-term loan, which has not yet been paid. While no money has been paid out, this charge has been incurred and must therefore be matched against the profits of that year.

1   i)   Cost of inventory is defined as cost of purchase, cost of conversion and other costs incurred in bringing the inventories to their present location and condition.

    ii)   Net realisable value is the estimated selling price in the ordinary course of business less the estimated costs of completion and the estimated costs necessary to make the sale.

2

	Inventory value £
Basic – cost	14,300
Standard – NRV (24,000 – 3,000)	21,000
Premium – cost	17,500
	52,800

3 i) FIFO

Date	Purchases		Issues		Balance	
	Qty	Unit cost £	Qty	Unit cost £	Qty	£
1 April	Opening balance				2,000	12,800
5 April	1,000 @ £7.00				1,000	7,000
					3,000	19,800
12 April			2,000 @ 6.40			
			500 @ 7.00			
			2,500		(2,500)	(16,300)
					500	3,500
17 April	2,000 @ £7.40				2,000	14,800
					2,500	18,300
26 April	1,500 @ £7.80				1,500	11,700
					4,000	30,000
30 April			500 @ £7.00			
			2,000 @ £7.40			
			500 @ £7.80			
			3,000		(3,000)	(22,200)
Closing inventory					1,000	7,800

	£
Sales (5,500 x £12)	66,000
Cost of sales (16,300 + 22,200)	(38,500)
Gross profit	27,500

ii) **AVCO**

Date		Movement £	Average cost £	Balance £
1 April	Opening balance	2,000	6.40	12,800
5 April	Purchases	1,000	7.00	7,000
		3,000	6.60	19,800
12 April	Sales	(2,500)	6.60	(16,500)
		500		3,300
17 April	Purchases	2,000	7.40	14,800
26 April	Purchases	1,500	7.80	11,700
		4,000	7.45	29,800
30 April	Sales	3,000	7.45	(22,350)
Closing inventory		1,000	7.45	7,450

	£
Sales (5,500 x £12)	66,000
Cost of sales (16,500 + 22,350)	(38,850)
Gross profit	27,150

4 i)

	£
Corporation tax	129,000
Less: over provision in previous year	(5,000)
Corporation tax charge	124,000

ii)

Corporation tax payable	129,000

5

- Permanent differences – items which are not allowed for corporation tax purposes. Example – business entertainment expenses.

- Temporary differences – differences between the carrying amount of an asset or liability in the balance sheet and its tax base (value for tax purposes). Examples include accelerated capital allowances and gains on revaluation of property.

6   **Income statement**

Tax expense

	£
Corporation tax	217,000
Add: underprovision in previous year	16,000
Add: transfer to deferred tax	
(180,000 – 150,000)	30,000
	263,000

Balance sheet – extract

	£
Current liabilities:	
Tax liabilities	217,000
Non-current liabilities:	
Deferred tax	180,000

7   i)   A provision should be made in the financial statements for this £4,000 as there would appear to be a constructive obligation to replace the goods.

ii)   This is an adjusting event after the balance sheet date as it is evidence of the net realisable value of the inventory at the balance sheet date. As such the closing inventory valuation in the financial statements should be reduced by £11,000 (£53,000 – 42,000).

iii) No provision should be made for this restructuring in the balance sheet as it has not been announced at the year end. A board decision is not enough to justify a provision.

iv)   This is an example of a contingent liability and as the possibility of a transfer of economic benefits is not remote the details should be disclosed in a note to the financial statements.

v)   This is a non-adjusting event after the balance sheet date and therefore no alteration is made to any figures in the financial statements. However as it is clearly material (almost doubling the issued share capital) it should be disclosed in a note to the financial statements.

8   MEMORANDUM

To: The Directors
           Franco Ltd

From: Accounting Technician   Date: 3 April 20X5

Accounting treatment

(i)   *Issue of shares at a premium*

       When shares are issued at an amount which exceeds their nominal value, the excess must be credited to a share premium account to which certain restrictions apply. Accordingly the required bookkeeping entries for such an issue would be:

DEBIT	Bank	£37,500	
CREDIT	Ordinary share capital (50p × 50,000)		£25,000
	Share premium (25p × 25,000)		£12,500

(ii)   This situation, where a customer goes into liquidation after the balance sheet date, is one which is specifically mentioned in IAS 10 Events after the balance sheet date as an 'adjusting event after the balance sheet date'. Adjusting events are described in the IAS as events after the balance sheet date which provide additional evidence of conditions existing at the balance sheet date, and consequently require the relevant amounts in the financial statements to be changed. In this case the debt of £30,000 would need to be written off. The bookkeeping entries would be:

DEBIT	Bad debts	£30,000	
CREDIT	Trade receivables		£30,000

(iii) The situation described here is covered by IAS 37 Provisions, contingent liabilities and contingent assets. A contingent asset is defined a 'a possible asset that arises from past events and whose existence will only be confirmed by the occurrence of one or more uncertain future events not wholly within the entities control'.

       It follows from the above definition that the probable inflow of £25,000 from the legal suit is a 'contingent asset'. IAS 37 states that if a contingent asset is probable, it should be disclosed by way of a note in the financial statements. It cannot be recognised or it would not be a contingent asset.

1 An item that meets the definition of an element should be recognised if:

- it is probable that any future economic benefit associated with the item will flow to or from the entity

- the item has a cost or value that can be measured with reliability.

2 This accounting treatment is not appropriate given the substance of the transaction.

The substance of the transaction would appear to be that National Bank has made a £1,000,000 loan to Birtles Ltd on the security of the building which is to be repaid in two years time with interest of £200,000 (£1,200,000 – 1,000,000). If this is the case then the property should remain in the balance sheet and a liability for a loan of £1,000,000 should also be recognised. There should be no profit on sale recorded as there is no true sale of the asset. Instead a portion of the interest of £200,000 should be charged to the income statement as interest on the loan.

3 i) A finance lease is a lease that transfers substantially all of the risks and rewards of ownership of an asset to the lessee.

ii) An operating lease is a lease other than a finance lease.

iii) An asset leased under a finance lease is recorded in the balance sheet as a non-current asset and is depreciated over the shorter of its useful life and the lease term. The asset is recognised at its fair value and a liability is set up for the same amount (being the amount owed to the lessor). Each lease payment is analysed into the capital element and the interest element. The income statement is charged with the interest element and the capital element reduces the liability in the balance sheet.

iv) For an operating lease no asset is recorded in the balance sheet. The lease payments are charged in full to the income statement.

v) The difference in accounting treatment between finance leases and operating leases reflects the very different commercial substance of the two types of transaction. An asset purchased under a finance lease is normally used by the lessee for most of the asset's life and it is very similar to owning the asset outright. Therefore the asset and related liability are shown in the balance sheet. However an asset under an operating lease is often only used by a particular lessee for a short part of its total useful life and the substance of the agreement is that it is a simple hire transaction.

4   All the following conditions must be satisfied.

- The entity has transferred the significant risks and rewards of ownership of the goods to the buyer

- The entity does not retain effective control over the goods sold

- The amount of revenue can be measured reliably

- It is probable that the economic benefits associated with the transaction will flow to the entity

- The costs incurred or to be incurred in respect of the transaction can be measured reliably. (IAS 18)

1 Gross profit $\quad\quad\quad$ = £425,000 – 280,000

$\quad\quad\quad\quad\quad\quad\quad\quad\quad$ = £145,000

Gross profit margin $\quad$ = $\dfrac{£145,000}{£425,000}$ x 100

$\quad\quad\quad\quad\quad\quad\quad\quad\quad$ = 34.1%

Net profit $\quad\quad\quad\quad$ = £145,000 – 98,000

$\quad\quad\quad\quad\quad\quad\quad\quad\quad$ = £47,000

Net profit margin $\quad\quad$ = $\dfrac{£47,000}{£425,000}$ x 100

$\quad\quad\quad\quad\quad\quad\quad\quad\quad$ = 11.1%

2 i) $\quad$ Gross profit margin $\quad\quad\quad$ = $\dfrac{522}{989}$ x 100

$\quad\quad\quad\quad\quad\quad\quad\quad\quad\quad\quad\quad$ = 52.8%

$\quad$ ii) $\quad$ Net profit margin $\quad\quad\quad\quad$ = $\dfrac{214}{989}$ x 100

$\quad\quad\quad\quad\quad\quad\quad\quad\quad\quad\quad\quad$ = 21.6%

$\quad$ iii) $\quad$ Return on capital employed $\quad$ = $\dfrac{214}{1,400}$ x 100

$\quad\quad\quad\quad\quad\quad\quad\quad\quad\quad\quad\quad$ = 15.3%

$\quad$ iv) $\quad$ Asset turnover $\quad\quad\quad\quad\quad$ = $\dfrac{989}{1,400}$

$\quad\quad\quad\quad\quad\quad\quad\quad\quad\quad\quad\quad$ = 0.71 times

v)   Return on equity $= \dfrac{180}{1,000} \times 100$

                                 $= 18\%$

vi)   Interest cover $= \dfrac{214}{34}$

                                 $= 6.3$ times

vii)   Gearing $= \dfrac{400}{1,400} \times 100$

                                 $= 28.6\%$

3   i)   Current ratio $= \dfrac{58,600+98,400}{86,200+6,300}$

                                 $= 1.7 : 1$

ii)   Quick (acid test) ratio $= \dfrac{98,400}{86,200+6,300}$

                                 $= 1.06 : 1$

iii)   Receivables days $= \dfrac{98,400}{772,400} \times 365$

                                 $= 46$ days

iv)   Inventory turnover $= \dfrac{507,400}{58,600}$

                                 $= 8.7$ times

v)   Inventory days $= \dfrac{58,600}{507,400} \times 365$

                                 $= 42$ days

vi)   Payables days $= \dfrac{86,200}{512,300} \times 365$

                                 $= 61$ days

NOTE: In many questions the purchases figure is not available, therefore the payables days are calculated based upon cost of sales. However, if the purchases figure is given this is a better figure to use for payables days.

4 i) In a highly geared company there is a relatively large amount of debt capital which must be serviced each period. This means that of the profits earned large amounts need to be paid out in the form of interest before any profits are available for the shareholders. This also means that profit levels must be high enough to cover the interest payments in each period. Therefore, from the shareholders' perspective, if profits fall then there is likely to be little or nothing left over for their dividend which can make the company appear risky. However it also holds true that if profits increase due to profitable investment of the debt finance then there is more available for the shareholders.

If a company has a large amount of debt finance then it might also be perceived as risky due to the fact that if the interest payments are not made on time to the debtholders they will have the right to put the company into liquidation.

ii) $$\text{Gearing} = \frac{\text{Debt}}{\text{Capital employed}}$$

$$\text{Debt to equity} = \frac{\text{Debt}}{\text{Share capital and reserves}}$$

5 Although ratio analysis can be a useful tool it does have its limitations.

- The financial statements used for the ratio analysis are based upon historical data which may be many months out of date – more recent information would tend to be more useful

- If the ratios are to be compared over a period of time the use of historical figures in the financial statements ignores any inflation element which could distort the trend of ratios over time

- Most of the ratios are based upon the closing balance sheet figures eg. ROCE, gearing, working capital ratios. These year end figures may not necessarily be indicative of the average figures for capital, debt, inventory etc. If this is the case then the ratio can be distorted and may not give a true picture of the general situation

- This problem is more intense in a seasonal business where the financial position may vary from time to time during the year

- If one or more companies are being compared to each other using ratio analysis the figures may not be truly comparable if the companies have different accounting policies. For example the balance sheet of a company which regularly revalues its assets will be very different from the balance sheet of a company that keeps its assets at historical cost

- The ratios that can be calculated are limited by the figures that actually appear in the financial statements which are only items that can be measured in monetary terms. Therefore important elements such as internally generated intangible assets and the human resources of the company are excluded.

6   i)   Rigby Ltd is operating on a high gross profit margin, relatively high net profit margin but a fairly low asset turnover. This indicates a low volume, high margin type of business. The ROCE is the same as that of Rialto Ltd but Rialto Ltd has low gross and net profit margins but high asset turnover indicating a high volume, low margin business.

In terms of working capital Rialto Ltd has a reasonable current ratio but low quick ratio indicating fairly large inventory levels although with inventory turnover of 10.3 times this inventory is being turned over much more rapidly than in Rigby Ltd. Rialto Ltd has virtually no receivables and both companies take a reasonable amount of credit from suppliers.

Rialto Ltd is more highly geared than Rigby Ltd but with interest cover of 5 times this would not appear to be a major problem.

ii)   From the ratios given it would appear that Rigby Ltd is the jeweller with relatively low revenue, high profit margins and slower inventory turnover. Rialto Ltd with higher, low margin revenue and no receivables would appear to be the supermarket.

REPORT

To: Shareholder
From: Accountant
Date: April 20X2
Subject: Garth Ltd – performance report

I have considered the financial statements for Garth Ltd for the two years ended 31 March 20X1 and 20X2. A number of key financial ratios have been calculated and these are included in the appendix to this report.

One key feature of the performance of Garth Ltd has been the increase in revenue of 20% in the two years. However despite the increased revenue the company has seen a marked fall in profitability. Return on capital employed has dropped significantly from 15% to 10%. Both the gross and net profit margins have declined over the period indicating that the increased revenue has been achieved by a drop in selling prices and increased operating expenses.

There has also been significant investment in property, plant and equipment with the book values showing a 34% increase. However with asset turnover falling over the two years it would not appear that this additional investment is as yet being put to fully profitable use within the business.

Both the current ratio and quick ratio have increased over the period indicating some possible problems with working capital management. If the individual elements of working capital are considered it can be seen that the problem area appears to be with receivables as the average period of credit being granted to customers has increased from 58 days to 85 days. This could indicate that the increase in revenue has been achieved not only by cutting prices but also by offering excessively generous credit terms to customers.

The increase in receivables days has not been matched by an increase in payables days as those have only increased by 11 days. Interestingly however in a period of revenue growth inventory days have fallen which may also indicate a problem if the manufacturing process cannot keep up with the sales demand.

In terms of overall financial position the investment in property, plant and equipment has been financed by taking out a further long term loan. The gearing level is now 41% of total capital employed which is not in itself excessively high but the interest cover has fallen to 3.4 indicating a certain increase of risk to the income of the shareholders.

In conclusion there would certainly appear to be some problems with the management of the company over the past two years. Despite the increased investment and revenue, profitability has fallen and receivables are increasingly a concern.

Appendix – Ratio Calculations

		Year ended 31 March	
		20X2	20X1
Gross profit margin	$=$	$\dfrac{183}{470} \times 100$	$\dfrac{166}{390} \times 100$
	$=$	39%	43%
Net profit margin	$=$	$\dfrac{183-97}{470} \times 100$	$\dfrac{166-73}{390} \times 100$
	$=$	18%	24%
Asset turnover	$=$	$\dfrac{470}{850}$	$\dfrac{390}{620}$
	$=$	0.55	0.63
Return on capital employed	$=$	$\dfrac{183-97}{850} \times 100$	$\dfrac{166-73}{620} \times 100$
	$=$	10%	15%
Current ratio	$=$	$\dfrac{162}{72}$	$\dfrac{119}{65}$
	$=$	2.25 : 1	1.8 : 1
Quick ratio	$=$	$\dfrac{126}{72}$	$\dfrac{82}{65}$
	$=$	1.75 : 1	1.3 : 1
Inventory days	$=$	$\dfrac{36}{287} \times 365$	$\dfrac{37}{224} \times 365$
	$=$	46 days	60 days
Receivables days	$=$	$\dfrac{110}{470} \times 365$	$\dfrac{62}{390} \times 365$
	$=$	85 days	58 days
Payables days	$=$	$\dfrac{41}{287} \times 365$	$\dfrac{25}{224} \times 365$
	$=$	52 days	41 days
Gearing	$=$	$\dfrac{350}{850} \times 100$	$\dfrac{150}{620} \times 100$
	$=$	41%	24%
Interest cover	$=$	$\dfrac{183-97}{25}$	$\dfrac{166-73}{14}$
	$=$	3.4 times	6.6 times

8   MEMO

To: The directors
              Dowango Ltd

From: AAT Student

Date: 30 April 20X6

Subject: Accounts of Dowango Ltd

i)   1)   It is certainly possible to show the land and buildings at valuation rather than cost. Although the normal basis for the preparation of financial statements should be historical cost principles, assets may be revalued.

      2)   The land would be shown at its valuation of £641,000 and the buildings at their valuation of £558,000. The difference between the net book value of the assets and their new valuation would be credited to a revaluation reserve, which is an undistributable reserve. The amounts to be credited to the revaluation reserve can be calculated as follows.

	Land £'000	Buildings £'000
Valuation	641	558
NBV	431	328
	210	230

      3)   Gearing is a measure of how much long-term finance is in the form of long-term debt. This may be measured as:

$$\frac{\text{Long term loans}}{\text{Total capital employed}} \times 100\%$$

            If the assets were revalued, the denominator of this ratio, ie total capital would increase by the amount credited to the revaluation reserve (£210,000 + 230,000 = £440,000). The gearing ratio would therefore reduce.

            It is possible that the lower gearing ratio may influence the bank's decision to lend the company the money to finance the acquisition. A lower gearing ratio means that the company is less risky from the bank's point of view.

      4)   In future years there will be an effect on the income statement. Depreciation would be calculated on the revalued amount, which is greater than historical cost. Thus the depreciation charge will be higher.

ii)   Because the investment is a current asset – it was purchased with a view to resale – it must be valued at the lower of purchase price and net realisable value. This is in accordance with the prudence concept, which states that profits should not be anticipated but that foreseeable losses should be provided for. As we can foresee a loss on the sale of the investment, it should be shown at its realisable value, the market value.

iii) The rule for valuation of inventories follows the prudence concept. It is set out in IAS 2 *Inventories*, which states that inventories should be valued at the lower of cost and net realisable value. Furthermore, the comparison of cost and net realisable value should be done on an item by item basis, not on the total of all inventories, although similar items may be grouped together. Applying this policy would lead us to value the undervalued items at a cost of £340,000 and the overvalued items at the sales price of £15,000. The effect of this is to reduce the overall value of inventory from £365,000 to £355,000 with the consequent effect of a £10,000 reduction in profit and assets.

Company A and Company B

The ratios may be calculated as follows.

	Company A	Company B
Return on capital employed	$\dfrac{200}{600+400} = 20\%$	$\dfrac{420}{1,700+1,100} = 15\%$
Net profit margin	$\dfrac{200}{800} = 25\%$	$\dfrac{420}{2,100} = 20\%$
Asset turnover	$\dfrac{800}{1,000} = 0.8$	$\dfrac{2,100}{2,800} = 0.75$

Other ratios which might be useful include the following. (Note that you were asked for only one of these ratios.)

	Company A	Company B
Gross profit margin	$\dfrac{360}{800} = 45\%$	$\dfrac{1,050}{2,100} = 50\%$
Expenses: sales	$\dfrac{160}{800} = 20\%$	$\dfrac{630}{2,100} = 30\%$

Most of the profitability ratios indicate that Company A would be the better one to target. Return on capital employed, net profit margin and asset turnover are all higher for Company A. However, if gross profit margin is calculated, the reverse is true, and Company B appears more profitable. This suggests that it is overheads rather than underlying profitability where Company B falls short, as is confirmed when one calculates the expenses to sales ratio. The question of which company to target is therefore not clear cut. If Company B were taken over and if a more efficient management were able to keep costs down, it might prove to be the more profitable in the long run.

9   REPORT

To: The Directors, Binns Ltd
From: A Technician
Date: 17 January 20X8
Subject: Financial statements of Gone Ltd

Introduction

The report analyses the financial statements of Gone Ltd with a view to assessing its suitability as a supplier for our company. The report shows certain key ratios covering profitability, liquidity and gearing. A comparison is made between 20X7 and 20X6 and also with the industry average for the year.

Summary of ratios

The ratios are summarised below. Calculations are shown in an appendix to this report.

	20X7	20X6
Return on capital employed	5.6%	11.1%
Gross profit percentage	39%	45%
Net profit percentage	11%	20.8%
Current ratio	1.2:1	2.1:1
Gearing	42.5%	20.5%

Profitability

Net profitability has declined in 20X7 in absolute terms as compared with 20X6 from £270,000 to £198,000, although gross profit has risen from £585,000 to £702,000. This is due to increased expenses – perhaps costs are not being kept under control. Revenue has increased. Possible an advertising campaign has been needed to expand the company's product range, although more information would be required to determine whether this is the case.

As regards profitability ratios, the 20X7 results show a decline as compared with 20X6. Return on capital employed and net profit margin are particularly worrying, having fallen by 50%. The 20X7 ratios for gross profit margin, net profit margin and return on capital employed are all below the industry average. In 20X6 the gross profit margin was above average, but this has now declined.

Overall the profitability figures are not particularly impressive. It is possible that some of this is due to the company's recent expansion – it has invested in non-current assets which have increased revenue but not profits as yet.

Liquidity

The current ratio is significantly worse in 20X7 than in 20X6 – 1.2 as opposed to 2.1. It is also much less in 20X7 than the industry average, whereas in 20X6 it was higher. This is a cause for concern, although the information does not show the components of current assets. If the fall is due to reduced inventory levels, this is less of a worry than a lower bank balance.

Gearing

As we are considering Gone Ltd as a potential supplier, we should be very wary of any factors which suggest that it may not be able to continue in business. High gearing is one such factor. Large debts carry risk of insolvency, and the company may have difficulty meeting interest payments.

The level of gearing has doubled in 20X7 and has gone from being comfortably below the industry average to worryingly above it. This, more than profitability or liquidity should be of concern to us. The company has used debt finance rather than equity to expand its asset base, but has not as yet increased profits.

Conclusion

On the basis of the above analysis, particularly as regards the level of gearing, I would recommend that we use an alternative supplier. It is possible that Gone Ltd's investment in new non-current assets will lead to a successful expansion of the business in the future, in which case we should reconsider our decision.

APPENDIX: CALCULATION OF RATIOS

		20X7			20X6
Return on capital employed	$\dfrac{198}{2{,}034+1{,}506}$	= 5.6%		$\dfrac{270}{1{,}938+500}$	= 11.1%
Gross profit percentage	$\dfrac{702}{1{,}800}$	= 39%		$\dfrac{585}{1{,}300}$	= 45%
Net profit percentage	$\dfrac{198}{1{,}800}$	= 11%		$\dfrac{270}{1{,}300}$	= 20.8%
Current ratio	$\dfrac{460}{383}$	= 1.2:1		$\dfrac{853}{406}$	= 2.1:1
Gearing	$\dfrac{1{,}506}{2{,}034+1{,}506}$	= 42.5%		$\dfrac{500}{1{,}938+500}$	= 20.5%

10 a) REPORT

To: The Directors, Animalets plc
From: A Technician
Date: 20 November 20X8

Performance and position of Superpet Ltd

As requested, I have analysed the performance and position of Superpet Ltd with special reference to selected accounting ratios. The calculation of the ratios is shown in the Appendix attached to this report.

General

Superpet is clearly expanding; both revenue and profit are up on 20X7. The company has invested in new non-current assets by increasing borrowing and issuing share capital.

Gross profit ratio

This has increased slightly from 53% in 20X7 to 58% in 20X8. This is due to a large increase in revenue and the fact that the cost of sales has not increased in proportion to the sales. Clearly, then, the company is not achieving increased sales at the expense of lower margins.

Current ratio

The current ratio has fallen slightly, but not significantly. It is still reasonably healthy. Sometimes expansion can give rise to overtrading, but this has not happened with Superpet.

Acid test ratio

This ratio, because it excludes inventories, may be regarded as a better indicator of the company's liquidity than the current ratio. Despite Superpet's expansion, the acid test ratio is healthy and shows a slight improvement on the previous year.

Gearing ratio

As mentioned above, Superpet has had to finance expansion by raising capital. Encouragingly, although the loan has increased, the gearing ratio, which was very low, has fallen. This is because there has been a proportionally greater increase in the equity (capital and reserves).

Conclusion

Overall, Superpet Ltd is expanding and healthy and the ratios do not give any cause for concern.

APPENDIX – CALCULATION OF RATIOS

	20X8		20X7	
Gross profit	$\dfrac{1,150}{2,000}$	= 58%	$\dfrac{800}{1,500}$	= 53%

Current ratio

	20X8		20X7	
$\dfrac{\text{Current assets}}{\text{Current liabilities}}$	$\dfrac{870}{670}$	= 1.3	$\dfrac{610}{448}$	= 1.4

Acid test ratio

	20X8		20X7	
$\dfrac{\text{Current assets – inventories}}{\text{Current liabilities}}$	$\dfrac{(870 - 350)}{670}$	= 0.8	$\dfrac{(610 - 300)}{448}$	= 0.7

Gearing ratio

	20X8		20X7	
$\dfrac{\text{Long – term loan}}{\text{Long – term loan} + \text{equity}}$	$\dfrac{100}{1,338}$	= 7%	$\dfrac{70}{800}$	= 9%

or

	20X8		20X7	
$\dfrac{\text{Long – term loan}}{\text{Equity}}$	$\dfrac{100}{1,238}$	= 8%	$\dfrac{70}{730}$	= 10%

b) SUPERPET LIMITED
RECONCILIATION OF OPERATING PROFIT
TO NET CASH FROM OPERATING ACTIVITIES

	£'000
Profit from operations	958
Depreciation	65
Profit on sale of asset	(5)
Increase in inventories	(50)
Increase in receivables	(150)
Increase in payables	122
Cash generated from operations	940
Interest paid	(10)
Taxation paid	(200)
Net cash from operating activities	730

11   Task 1

AAT Student
ABC Accountant
Blank Road
Blank Town

24 June 20X3

Dear Ms Grieg

Performance of Gint Ltd

As requested I am writing to give you advice on the performance and financial position of Gint Ltd. You should find this advice useful in deciding whether to lend money to the company. I have based my analysis around a number of key ratios, shown in an appendix to this letter.

Current ratio

This is a liquidity ratio, showing the extent to which a company's current liabilities are covered by current assets. Generally speaking, a current ratio of less than one gives cause for concern – if a company cannot pay its creditors, it may go out of business.

Gint Ltd's current ratio is healthy and has shown an increase on the previous year. However, the cash balance has gone down, so the liquidity is not as good as it might be.

Quick ratio/acid test

The quick ratio shows how many assets, excluding inventories, are available to meet the current liabilities. Inventories are excluded because it is not always readily convertible into cash. The quick ratio or acid test is therefore a better indicator of a company's true liquidity than the current ratio which does not exclude inventories.

Gint's ratio has declined. In 20X2 it had almost enough current assets (excluding inventories) to cover its current liabilities. In 20X3, however, there is a slight shortfall. The company would be advised to get a cash injection in order to avoid liquidity problems.

Gearing ratio

As we are considering lending money to Gint Ltd, we should be very wary of any factors which suggest that it may not be able to continue in business. High gearing is one such factor. Large debts carry risk of insolvency and the company may have difficulty meeting interest payments.

The gearing ratio can be calculated in two ways: debt/equity and debt/capital employed. Gint's ratio, whichever way it is calculated, has risen slightly compared with 20X2. However, it is still low and therefore the company is not risky in this respect.

Interest cover

The interest cover ratio shows whether a company is earning enough profits before interest and tax to pay its interest costs comfortably, or whether its interest costs are high in relation to the size of its profits. Low levels of cover may make it difficult for a company to borrow more funds.

Gint's interest cover has increased from last year and is healthy.

Conclusion

This is a growing company with healthy increase in revenue and profits. The company would not have problems meeting interest payments on a loan, and gearing is low. Liquidity ratios give some cause for concern: much of the company's working capital is tied up in inventories, rather than more liquid assets. However, a cash injection by way of a loan would ease Gint's liquidity problems and enable it to grow. In conclusion, on the basis of my analysis, I would recommend that a loan should be made to Gint Ltd.

Yours sincerely

AAT Student

APPENDIX: CALCULATION OF RATIOS

	20X3	20X2
Current ratio	$\dfrac{1,663}{563} = 2.9$	$\dfrac{1,301}{510} = 2.6$
Quick ratio/acid test	$\dfrac{506}{563} = 0.9$	$\dfrac{585}{510} = 1.1$
Gearing ratio		
Debt/equity	$\dfrac{600}{4,872} = 12.3\%$	$\dfrac{500}{4,632} = 10.8\%$
Debt/capital employed	$\dfrac{600}{5,472} = 11.0\%$	$\dfrac{500}{5,132} = 9.7\%$
Interest cover	$\dfrac{552}{46} = 12$	$\dfrac{410}{41} = 10$

Task 2

a)
Equity	= share capital and retained earnings	= £4,872
Assets	= plant, property and equipment plus current assets	= £6,035
Liabilities	= current liabilities plus long-term loan	= £1,163

b)   The accounting equation is as follows.

Assets	less	liabilities	=	equity
£6,035	–	£1,163	=	£4,872

REPORT

To: Michael Beacham

From: Accounting Technician

Subject: Interpretation of the ratios of Goodall Ltd

Date: October 20X3

As requested, I have analysed the financial performance and position of Goodall Ltd for 20X2 and 20X3. This analysis has been based on the ratios calculated by your financial adviser, which have been compared with industry averages.

Gearing ratio

This ratio is often used as a measure of the risk involved in investing in or lending to a business. It measures the proportion of a company's debt (normally long term borrowings) compared to its total capital employed. The ratio has risen from 58% in 20X2 to 67% in 20X3 and is considerably higher than the industry average of 41%. This suggests that Goodall Ltd is a much riskier investment than other businesses in its industry sector and that the position is deteriorating.

Interest cover

This ratio measures the extent to which a company's interest payments are covered by its operating profit. Interest cover has decreased by almost half in the period, so that in 20X3 the company's operating profit was only very slightly more than its interest payable. This is very low indeed compared with the industry average of 4.6. The company appears to be generating much less profit relative to interest than other businesses in the industry.

Quick ratio/Acid test

This ratio measures the company's ability to meet its current liabilities from cash and from converting debtors into cash. Again, this ratio has decreased in the two year period and it is now much lower than the industry average of 1.1. At its last balance sheet date its current liabilities were twice as great as its 'quick' current assets, suggesting that Goodall Ltd has significant liquidity problems compared with other companies in the sector.

Return on equity

This ratio measures the profit available to equity shareholders that is generated by the use of equity finance (ordinary shares and reserves). Again, this ratio has fallen sharply over the period, suggesting that there is less profit available for equity shareholders. This means that they are unlikely to receive much immediate return on their investment (in the form of dividends) and that there is little profit available for reinvestment in the company to generate better returns in future. The return on equity of Goodall Ltd is considerably lower than the industry average of 19%, which means that the company is much less likely to attract equity investors than other companies within the sector.

Conclusion

Goodall Ltd is already very highly geared, its interest cover is deteriorating and it appears to be suffering liquidity problems. All these things suggest that there would be considerable risk in lending money to this company, unless the loan is almost certain to generate increased profits in the short term. It is quite possible that the company will be unable to meet its interest payments in future as neither the profits nor the cash may be available. Return on equity is very low, which means that the company is unlikely to be able to raise additional finance from investors. On the basis of the limited information provided, it would not be advisable to make a loan to this company.

answers to chapter 10: THE CONSOLIDATED BALANCE SHEET

1   A company is a subsidiary of another (the parent) if that other company can control it. IAS 27 states that:

   ■   control is presumed to exist where the parent owns more than half the voting power of an entity; and control also exists when the parent owns half or less of the voting power of an entity when there is:

      -   power over more than half of the voting rights by virtue of an agreement with other investors;

      -   power to govern the financial and operating policies of the entity under a statute or an agreement;

      -   power to appoint or remove the majority of the members of the board of directors; or

      -   power to cast the majority of votes at meetings of the board of directors.

2   **Consolidated balance sheet as at 31 March 20X2**

	£
Goodwill (W)	5,000
Property, plant and equipment (200,000 + 80,000)	280,000
Net current assets (40,000 + 30,000)	70,000
	355,000
Share capital	250,000
Retained earnings (W)	105,000
	355,000

Workings

Goodwill

	£	£
Cost of investment		100,000
Less: net assets acquired		
Share capital	50,000	
Retained earnings	45,000	
		(95,000)
Goodwill		5,000

Consolidated retained earnings reserve

	£	£
P Ltd		90,000
S Ltd		
At 31 March 20X2	60,000	
At acquisition	(45,000)	
		15,000
		105,000

3   Consolidated balance sheet as at 31 December 20X1

	£
Goodwill (W)	20,000
Property, plant and equipment (800,000 + 400,000)	1,200,000
Net current assets (70,000 + 75,000)	145,000
	1,365,000
Share capital	800,000
Retained earnings (W)	446,250
	1,246,250
Minority interest (W)	118,750
	1,365,000

Workings

Goodwill

	£	£
Cost of investment		350,000
Less: net assets acquired		
Share capital	200,000	
Retained earnings	240,000	
Group share 75%	440,000	330,000
Goodwill		20,000

Consolidated retained earnings reserve

	£	£
X Ltd		420,000
Y Ltd		
At 31 December 20X1	275,000	
At acquisition	(240,000)	
Group share 75%	35,000	26,250
		446,250

Minority interest

	£
Share capital	200,000
Retained earnings	275,000
	475,000
Minority share 25%	118,750

4   Consolidated balance sheet as at 30 April 20X2

	£
Goodwill (W)	30,000
Property, plant and equipment (W)	2,429,200
Net current assets (240,000 + 85,000)	325,000
	2,784,200
Share capital	2,000,000
Retained earnings	784,200
	2,784,200

Workings

Goodwill

	£	£
Cost of investment		850,000
Net assets acquired		
Share capital	300,000	
Retained earnings	480,000	
Fair value adjustment (240,000 – 200,000)	40,000	
		820,000
Goodwill		30,000

Consolidated property, plant and equipment

	£	£
A Ltd		1,640,000
B Ltd		
Book value	750,000	
Fair value adjustment	40,000	
Additional depreciation (£40,000 x 2%)	(800)	
		789,200
		2,429,200

Consolidated retained earnings reserve

	£	£
A Ltd		730,000
B Ltd		
At balance sheet date (535,000 + 40,000 – 800)	574,200	
At acquisition (480,000 + 40,000)	(520,000)	
		54,200
		784,200

5   Consolidated balance sheet as at 31 March 20X2

	£	£
Non-current assets		
Property, plant and equipment (1,000,000 + 625,000)		1,625,000
Current assets		
Inventories (60,000 + 30,000)	90,000	
Receivables (80,000 – 15,000 + 50,000)	115,000	
Cash (10,000 + 5,000)	15,000	
		220,000
Total assets		1,845,000
Current liabilities (50,000 + 45,000 – 15,000)		80,000
Net current assets		140,000
Net assets		1,765,000
Equity		
Share capital		1,000,000
Retained earnings		632,000
Attributable to equity holders of the parent		1,632,000
Minority interest		133,000
		1,765,000

Workings

Goodwill

	£	£
Cost of investment		460,000
Less: group share of net assets acquired		
Share capital	300,000	
Retained earnings	200,000	
Group share 80%	500,000	400,000
Goodwill		60,000
Less: amounts written off		(60,000)
		–

Consolidated retained earnings reserve

	£	£
C Ltd		560,000
D Ltd	365,000	
Less: pre-acquisition	(200,000)	
Group share 80%	165,000	132,000
Less: goodwill written off		(60,000)
		632,000

Minority interest

	£	£
Share capital		300,000
Retained earnings		365,000
		665,000
Minority share 20%		133,000

6 Consolidated balance sheet as at 31 December 20X2

	£
Goodwill (W)	49,000
Property, plant and equipment (600,000 + 380,000)	980,000
Net current assets (80,000 + 35,000)	115,000
	1,144,000
Share capital	600,000
Retained earnings (W)	378,000
	978,000
Minority interest (W)	166,000
	1,144,000

Workings

Goodwill

	£	£
Cost of investment		250,000
Net assets acquired		
Share capital	150,000	
Retained earnings	185,000	
Group share 60%	335,000	201,000
Goodwill		49,000

Consolidated retained earnings reserve

	£	£
F Ltd		330,000
G Ltd	265,000	
Less: pre-acquisition	(185,000)	
Group share 60%	80,000	48,000
		378,000

Minority interest

	£	£
Share capital		150,000
Retained earnings		265,000
		415,000
Minority share 40%		166,000

7   **Consolidated balance sheet as at 31 March 20X2**

	£	£
Non-current assets:		
Goodwill (W)		52,000
Property, plant and equipment (580,000 + 280,000)		860,000
		912,000
Current assets:		
Inventory (40,000 + 20,000)		60,000
Receivables (50,000 + 30,000 – 20,000)		60,000
Cash (5,000 + 2,000)		7,000
		127,000
Total assets		1,039,000
Current liabilities (55,000 + 32,000 - 20,000)		67,000
Net current assets		60,000
Net assets		972,000
Equity:		
Share capital		600,000
Retained earnings (W)		312,000
Attributable to equity holders of the parent		912,000
Minority interest (W)		60,000
		972,000

Workings

Goodwill

	£	£
Cost of investment		260,000
Net assets acquired		
Share capital	200,000	
Retained earnings	60,000	
Group share	260,000	208,000
Goodwill		52,000

Consolidated retained earnings reserve

	£	£
M Ltd		280,000
N Ltd	100,000	
Less: pre acquisition	(60,000)	
Group share 80%	40,000	32,000
		312,000

Minority interest

	£	£
Share capital		200,000
Retained earnings		100,000
		300,000
Minority share 20%		60,000

8 CALCULATION OF GOODWILL ON CONSOLIDATION
ARISING ON ACQUISITION OF MACNEAL LTD

	£'000	£'000
Cost of investment		5,000
Net assets acquired		
Share capital	1,200	
Share premium	800	
Revaluation reserve (W1)	1,000	
Retained earnings	2,800	
	5,800	
Group share (W2): 75%		4,350
		650

Workings

1 *Revaluation reserve*

	£'000
Fair value of non-current assets	5,844
Book value of non-current assets	4,844
Revaluation reserve	1,000

2 *Group share*

$$\frac{900}{1,200} \text{ shares} = 75\%$$

9   NORMAN LIMITED
CONSOLIDATED BALANCE SHEET AS AT 31 MARCH 20X3

	£'000
Non-current assets:	
Intangible assets: Goodwill (460 − 46)(W3)	414
Property, plant and equipment (12,995 + 1,755 + 400)	15,150
	15,564
Current assets:	
Inventories (3,586 + 512)	4,098
Trade and other receivables (2,193 + 382)	2,575
Cash and cash equivalents (84 + 104)	188
	6,861
Total assets	22,425
Current liabilities:	
Trade payables (1,920 + 273)	2,193
Tax liabilities (667 + 196)	863
	3,056
Net current assets	3,805
Non-current liabilities: Long-term loan	400
Total liabilities	3,456
Net assets	18,969
Equity:	
Share capital	2,000
Retained earnings (W5)	16,398
Attributable to equity holders of the parent	18,398
Minority interest (W4)	571
	18,969

Workings

1   *Group structure*

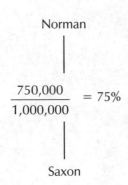

Norman

$$\frac{750,000}{1,000,000} = 75\%$$

Saxon

2   *Revaluation reserve: Saxon*

	£'000
Fair value of property, plant and equipment	2,047
Book value of property, plant and equipment	1,647
Revaluation reserve	400

3   *Goodwill*

	£'000	£'000
Cost of investment		1,978
Fair value of net assets acquired		
Share capital	1,000	
Share premium	200	
Revaluation reserve	400	
Reserves at acquisition	424	
	2,024	
Group share 75%		1,518
Goodwill		460
Impairment loss (10%)		(46)
		414

4   *Minority interests*

	£000
Saxon's net assets per question at 31 March 2003	1,884
Add revaluation reserve	400
	2,284

∴ Minority interests = £2,284,000 x 25% = £571,000

5   *Reserves*

	£'000	£'000
Norman		16,249
Less goodwill written off		(46)
		16,203
Saxon	684	
Less: pre-acquisition	(424)	
	260	
Group share 75%		195
		16,398

10 a) **Goodwill**

	£'000	£'000
Cost of investment		3,510
Net assets acquired:		
Share capital	2,000	
Share premium	1,000	
Retained earnings	1,350	
Fair value adjustment (4,455 - 4,055)	400	
	4,750	
Group share (60%)		(2,850)
		660
Less: impairment (10%)		(66)
		594

Working

Group structure

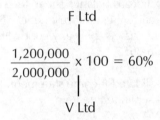

F Ltd

$$\frac{1,200,000}{2,000,000} \times 100 = 60\%$$

V Ltd

b) **Minority interest**

	£'000
Net assets at 31 March 20X3	4,770
Fair value adjustment	400
	5,170
Minority share (40%)	2,068

c) **Consolidated retained earnings reserve**

	£'000	£'000
Fertwangler Ltd		5,610
Voncarryon Ltd:		
At 31 March 20X3	1,770	
At acquisition	(1,350)	
	420	
Group share (60%)		252
Impairment of goodwill		(66)
		5,796

d) i) **Associate**

An associate is an entity over which an investor has significant influence and that is neither a subsidiary nor a joint venture.

Significant influence is the power to participate in the financial and operating policy decisions of an entity.

When an investor exercises significant influence it is actively involved in the affairs of an investee and it influences major decisions, for example on strategy and dividend policy.

On the basis of the information given, Triumphara Ltd appears to fall within this definition. A shareholding of 40% normally gives significant influence, unless there are other major shareholdings that would prevent this.

Treatment in the consolidated financial statements

In the consolidated balance sheet, the group's investment in the associate is shown under non-current asset investments. This is calculated as the group's share of the associate's net assets, plus any goodwill arising on the acquisition that has not yet been written off.

In the consolidated income statement, the group's share of the associate's profit is shown as a separate line item.

ii) **Inter-company sales**

The consolidated financial statements show the financial performance and position of the group as a single entity. When a company makes a sale to another company in the same group it records sales revenue and a profit, but from the point of view of the group no sale has taken place and no profit is earned until the goods are sold on to a third party.

Therefore the effect of inter-group sales must be removed from the consolidated financial statements:

- Revenue and cost of sales are both reduced by the amount of the inter-company sales.

- Where any goods purchased from another group company remain in inventory at the year-end, closing inventory is reduced to take account of unrealised profit. This affects both the balance sheet and cost of sales.

- Any inter-company balances (receivables and payables) should also be eliminated.

1   Consolidated income statement for the year ended 31 March 20X2

	£
Revenue (460,000 + 221,000)	681,000
Cost of sales (270,000 + 132,000)	402,000
Gross profit	279,000
Operating expenses (87,000 + 43,000)	130,000
Profit before tax	149,000
Tax (30,000 + 12,000)	42,000
Profit for the year	107,000

Attributable to:

	£
Equity holders of the parent	96,800
Minority interests (30% x 34,000)	10,200
	107,000

2   Consolidated income statement for the year ended 30 April 20X2

	£
Revenue (694,000 + 372,000 – 120,000)	946,000
Cost of sales (416,000 + 223,000 – 120,000)	519,000
Gross profit	427,000
Operating expenses (174,000 + 75,000)	249,000
Profit before tax	178,000
Tax (26,000 + 19,000)	45,000
Profit for the year	133,000

Attributable to:

	£
Equity holders of the parent	111,000
Minority interests (40% x 55,000)	22,000
	133,000

3   Consolidated income statement for the year ending 31 December 20X1

	£
Revenue (386,000 + 147,000 – 50,000)	483,000
Cost of sales (250,000 + 95,000 – 50,000)	295,000
Gross profit	188,000
Operating expenses (77,000 + 29,000)	106,000
Profit before tax	82,000
Tax (16,000 + 6,000)	22,000
Profit for the year	60,000

Attributable to:

	£
Equity holders of the parent	53,200
Minority interests (17,000 × 40%)	6,800
	60,000

4   In the consolidated balance sheet the group share of the net assets of the associate is shown as a non-current asset investment. This figure includes any goodwill. The consolidated reserves include the group share of the associate's post acquisition profit.

In the consolidated income statement the group share of the associate's profit after tax is shown above profit before tax.

The reason for using the equity method for accounting for an associate is to recognise the significant influence that the group has on the associate. Just to show the associate as an investment at cost with dividend income in the income statement would not reflect this significant influence. Equally the associate should not be consolidated like a subsidiary as the parent does not have control of an associate. Therefore the equity method of accounting is used as a method of accounting in the middle of these two extremes.

5   Consolidated balance sheet as at 31 March 20X2

	£
Non-current assets:	
Property, plant and equipment	410,000
Investment in associate (W)	28,250
	438,250
Current assets:	
Inventory	61,000
Trade and other receivables	66,000
Cash	8,000
	135,000
Total assets	573,250
Current liabilities:	
Trade and other payables	102,000
Net current assets	33,000
Net assets	471,250
Equity:	
Share capital	300,000
Retained earnings (W)	171,250
	471,250

Consolidated income statement for the year ended 31 March 20X2

	£
Revenue	410,000
Cost of sales	(287,000)
Gross profit	123,000
Operating expenses	(84,000)
Share of profit of associate (25% x 17,000)	4,250
Profit before tax	43,250
Tax	(12,000)
Profit for the year	31,250

Workings

Goodwill

	£	£
Cost of investment		24,000
Share of net assets acquired		
Share capital	40,000	
Retained earnings	40,000	
Group share 25%	80,000	20,000
Goodwill		4,000

	£
Group share of the net assets of the associate	
at balance sheet date (25% x £97,000)	24,250
Goodwill	4,000
	28,250

Retained earnings reserve at the balance sheet date

	£
Gilbert group	167,000
Group share of associate's post acquisition	
profits (25% x (57,000 – 40,000))	4,250
	171,250

6   The answer is no. IAS 27 states that **all** material subsidiaries must be included in the consolidated financial statements.

7   a)   If Animalets were to purchase 30% of the shares of Superpet, giving the directors significant influence over Superpet, the latter would be an associate of Animalets. The accounting treatment would then follow IAS 28 and is known as equity accounting.

        Consolidated income statement

        Animalets' share of the profit after tax of Superpet should be included as a line item.

        Consolidated balance sheet

        i)   Original cost of investment, plus;
        ii)   Group's share of profits earned since acquisition not distributed as dividends.

        This is included under non-current assets and described as 'investment in associate'.

   b)   If Animalets were to purchase a 75% stake, together with control, Superpet would be a subsidiary of Animalets. In the consolidated accounts, the income and expenditure and the assets and liabilities of Superpet would be added on a line-by-line basis to those of Animalets under the purchase method. The remaining 25% of the shares not acquired by Animalets would be shown as a minority interest.

PRACTICE EXAM 1

HAYDN PLC

ANSWERS

ANSWERS

SECTION 1

PART A

Task 1.1

Haydn plc
Consolidated balance sheet at 30 September 20X5

	£'000
Non-current assets	
Intangible assets: goodwill (W2)	13,370
Property, plant and equipment (88,301 + 45,523 + 4,000) (W2))	137,824
	151,194
Current assets:	
Inventory	32,066
Trade and other receivables	13,872
Cash and cash equivalents	1,429
	47,367
Total assets	198,561
Current liabilities:	
Trade and other payables	16,671
Accruals	3,975
Tax liabilities	2,546
	23,192
Net current assets	24,175
Non-current liabilities:	
Long-term loans	57,000
Total liabilities	80,192
Net assets	118,369
Equity	
Share capital	30,000
Share premium	20,000
Retained earnings (W3)	48,997
Equity attributable to equity holders of the parent	98,997
Minority interests (W4)	19,372
Total equity	118,369

Workings

1   *Group structure*

Haydn plc owns 60% (3,000/5,000) of Seek Ltd.

2   *Goodwill*

	£'000	£'000
Cost of investment		39,500
Less: net assets acquired:		
Share capital	5,000	
Share premium	2,000	
Retained earnings	32,550	
Fair value adjustment (42,500 - 38,500)	4,000	
	43,550	
Group share (60%)		(26,130)
		13,370

3   *Retained earnings*

	£'000	£'000
Haydn plc		46,069
Seek Ltd: At balance sheet date	37,430	
At acquisition	(32,550)	
	4,880	
Group share (60%)		2,928
		48,997

4   *Minority interest*

	£'000
Net assets at balance sheet date	44,430
Fair value adjustment	4,000
	48,430
MI share (40%)	19,372

Task 1.2

The accounting treatment of goodwill arising on consolidation is covered by IFRS 3 *Business combinations*. This states that goodwill must be recognised as an asset and carried in the consolidated balance sheet at cost. Amortisation of goodwill is prohibited. Instead, it should be tested for impairment annually or more often if there is any indication that it may have become impaired. The impairment test is carried out in accordance with IAS 36 *Impairment of assets*. Any impairment loss is recognised immediately in the income statement.

Part B

Task 1.3

Journal entries

			£'000	£'000
1	Dr	Cash at bank (2,000 x £1.50)	3,000	
	Cr	Share capital		2,000
	Cr	Share premium (2,000 x £0.50)		1,000
2	Dr	Inventory (balance sheet)	8,731	
	Cr	Inventory (income statement)		8,731
3	Dr	Cash at bank	1,500	
	Cr	Property, plant and equipment: accum depn	1,250	
	Cr	Disposals		2,300
	Dr	Disposals		450
4	Dr	Tax expense	3,948	
	Cr	Tax liability		3,948
5	Dr	Interest expense (15,000 x 8% x 6/12)	600	
	Cr	Interest accrual		600

Task 1.4

Moatsart Ltd
Income statement for the year ended 30 September 20X5

	£'000
Continuing operations	
Revenue (70,613 - 2,372)	68,241
Cost of sales (W1)	(34,803)
Gross profit	33,438
Distribution costs	(12,386)
Administrative expenses	(7,115)
Profit on disposal of property, plant and equipment	450
Profit from operations	14,387
Finance costs (600 + 600)	(1,200)
Profit before tax	13,187
Tax	(3,948)
Profit for the period from continuing operations attributable to equity holders	9,239

Balance sheet at 31 March 20X5

	£'000
Non-current assets:	
Property, plant and equipment (W2)	57,384
Investments	4,000
	61,384
Current assets:	
Inventory	8,731
Trade and other receivables (W3)	8,475
Cash and cash equivalents (1,535 + 3,000 + 1,500)	6,035
	23,241
Total assets	84,625
Current liabilities:	
Trade and other payables (W4)	10,181
Tax liabilities	3,948
	14,129
Net current assets	9,112
Non-current liabilities:	
Long-term loan	15,000
Total liabilities	29,129
Net assets	55,496
Equity:	
Share capital (8,000 + 2,000)	10,000
Share premium (3,000 + 1,000)	4,000
Revaluation reserve	2,500
Retained earnings (W5)	38,996
	55,496

Workings

1	Cost of sales	£'000
	Opening inventory	7,454
	Purchases	37,543
	Less: returns outwards	(1,463)
	Less: closing inventory	(8,731)
		34,803

2   Property, plant and equipment

	Cost	Acc depn	Total
	£'000	£'000	£'000
Per TB	84,856	26,422	48,434
Less: disposal	(2,300)	(1,250)	(1,050)
	82,556	25,172	57,384

3 **Trade and other receivables** £'000

Trade receivables 8,754

Less: provision for doubtful debts (682)

8,072

Prepayments 403

8,475

4 **Trade and other payables** £'000

Trade payables 8,939

Accruals per TB 642

Interest accrual 600

10,181

5 **Retained earnings** £'000

Retained earnings per TB 32,157

Add: profit for the year 9,239

Less: dividends paid (2,400)

38,996

Task 1.5

a) Under the going concern basis, a company prepares its financial statements on the assumption that it is a going concern, that is, it will continue in operation for the foreseeable future. This means that assets are measured at amounts that are relevant to the way in which the company will use them in its ongoing operations, rather than at their 'break up' values (the amounts for which they could be sold immediately as individual items).

Under the accruals basis of accounting, the effects of transactions and other events are recognised when they occur rather than when cash is received or paid. They are recorded in the accounting records and reported in the financial statements in the period to which they relate.

b) Where there is a standard that specifically applies to a transaction, event or other condition, that standard, and any interpretation guidance issued with it, determines the accounting policy.

In the absence of a standard that specifically applies to a transaction, other event or condition, management should use its judgement in developing and applying an accounting policy that results in information that is:

- relevant to the decision making needs of the user; and
- reliable, in that the financial statements

  - represent faithfully the financial position, financial performance and cash flows of the entity;

  - reflect the economic substance of transactions and not merely the legal form

  - are neutral (free from bias)

  - are prudent; and

  - are complete in all material respects.

Part C

Task 1.6

Bateoven Ltd
Reconciliation of profit from operations to net cash from operating activities

	£'000
Profit from operations	312
Adjustments for: depreciation	3,570
Operating cash flows before movements in working capital	3,882
Increase in inventories (3,670 - 3,162)	(508)
Increase in trade receivables (1,777 - 1,306)	(471)
Decrease in trade payables (975 - 646)	(329)
Cash generated from operations	2,574
Interest paid	(560)
Income taxes paid	(1,284)
Net cash from operating activities	730

Task 1.7

Sender's address

The Directors of Bateoven Ltd
Address

December 20X5

Dear Directors

Sources and uses of cash

As requested, I set out my comments on the way in which Bateoven Ltd has generated and used cash during the year ended 30 September 20X5.

Sources of cash

The company experienced a total operating cash inflow of £3,882,000. Approximately one third of this inflow was absorbed by movements in working capital, leaving net cash generated from operations of £2,574,000.

The company raised additional cash of £5,000,000 from an issue of ordinary shares. It also increased its long term loan by £4,100,000.

Uses of cash

The company spent cash of £9,138,000 on the purchase of new property, plant and equipment. This expenditure was largely covered by the additional cash of £9,100,000 raised from the share issue and the increase in long term debt. This was presumably the reason for raising the additional finance.

There were also routine operating cash outflows of £560,000 in respect of Interest on the long term loan and £1,284,000 in respect of corporation tax. These were covered by cash generated from operations.

The company also paid a dividend of £2,000,000 on its ordinary shares. The remaining cash generated from operations was insufficient to cover the dividend payment. This appears to be the main reason why cash decreased by £1,308,000 during the year.

Further comments

Two areas give some cause for concern. The first is the extent to which cash from operations has been absorbed by changes in working capital. Inventories, trade receivables and trade payables have all increased significantly during the year and it is possible that cash has been tied up unnecessarily in this way.

The second is the payment of what appears to be a very large dividend in relation to profit from operations for the year. The company has to pay interest on the loan and must meet its tax liabilities, but it is not legally obliged to pay a dividend. (It should be noted that the company made a loss before tax of £248,000 for the year ended 30 September 20X5, although the dividend probably relates to 20X4 when profits may have been higher.)

However, although the company now has a significant amount of long term debt, it still has a positive cash balance of £93,000, so it is unlikely to experience severe liquidity problems in the very short term.

I hope that this analysis has been helpful to you. Please do not hesitate to contact me should you require any further assistance.

Yours sincerely

SECTION 2

Task 2.1

REPORT

To: John Brams
From: Accounting technician
Subject: Financial performance of Ma Leer Ltd
Date: December 20X5

As requested, I have analysed the financial performance of Ma Leer Ltd, based on the ratios provided.

a) **Formulae used to calculate the ratios**

Return on capital employed

$$\frac{\text{Profit from operations}}{\text{Capital employed}}$$

Net profit ratio

$$\frac{\text{Profit from operations}}{\text{Sales revenue}}$$

Gross profit ratio

$$\frac{\text{Gross profit}}{\text{Sales revenue}}$$

Expenses ratio

$$\frac{\text{Operating expenses}}{\text{Sales revenue}}$$

Asset turnover

$$\frac{\text{Sales revenue}}{\text{Capital employed}}$$

Inventory turnover

$$\frac{\text{Inventory}}{\text{Cost of sales}} \times 365$$

Receivables turnover

$$\frac{\text{Trade receivables}}{\text{Sales}} \times 365$$

Payables turnover

$$\frac{\text{Trade payables}}{\text{Cost of sales}} \times 365$$

b) **Improvement and deterioration**

Return on capital employed has deteriorated

The ratio shows the return (profit) earned by the company on its capital, that is, the net assets that it uses in its operations. The company earned a return of 15% on capital employed in 20X5, compared with a higher return of 19% in 20X4.

Net profit ratio has deteriorated

This ratio is a measure of a company's overall profitability. It expresses profit from operations as a percentage of sales. The net profit ratio has fallen from 22% in 20X4 to 20% in 20X5, meaning that the company has become slightly less profitable.

Gross profit ratio has improved

This ratio shows the profit margin that a company makes on its trading activities by showing its gross profit as a percentage of sales. The ratio has risen from 42% in 20X4 to 46% in 20X5, meaning that the company's trading activities have become more profitable.

Expenses ratio has deteriorated

This calculation shows that in 20X5 the company's operating expenses were slightly higher compared with its sales revenue than they were in 20X4. Operating expenses reduce the company's profit.

Asset turnover has deteriorated

The asset turnover ratio shows how much sales revenue a company has generated in relation to its assets (or capital employed). It can be seen as a measure of the efficiency with which the assets are used by management. Whereas in 2004 the company generated 86p in revenue for every £1 of the company's assets, it only generated 75p for every £1 of assets in 20X5.

Inventory turnover has deteriorated

The inventory turnover ratio shows the average period in days for which the company holds an item of inventory. This was 93 days in 20X5 compared with 71 days in 20X4. It is desirable to hold inventory for as short a time as possible. Holding inventory absorbs cash because cash has been paid to purchase items but no cash will be received until they are sold.

Receivables turnover has deteriorated

The receivables turnover ratio shows that the average period taken to collect amounts receivable from customers was 47 days in 20X4, but this had risen to 54 days in 20X5. This suggests that the company has become less efficient in collecting receivables.

Payables turnover has deteriorated

The payables turnover ratio shows that the average period taken to pay suppliers was 29 days in 20X4 but that this had fallen to 25 days in 20X5. Paying suppliers more quickly than before reduces the amounts of cash available to the company.

c) **Overall change in financial performance**

Return on capital employed has deteriorated significantly during the year. This suggests that investors are not obtaining as a good a return on the capital that they have invested as in previous years. There are two reasons for this. The company is slightly less profitable in 20X5 than it was in 20X4. In addition the company is not generating as much revenue from its capital (assets) as in the previous year.

The fall in the net profit ratio has occurred despite the fact that the company's gross profit margin has actually improved significantly in the year. The most likely reason for the deterioration in the net profit percentage is shown by the expenses ratio. Operating expenses (such as administrative expenses) have risen disproportionately when compared with sales.

The three working capital ratios (inventory turnover, receivables turnover and payables turnover) have all worsened. This means that there has probably been a significant increase in the amount of cash 'tied up' in working capital, with an adverse effect on te company's cash flow.

The overall picture is of a company which is not being managed as well as in previous years. The fact that the company's gross profit margin has increased indicates that there is nothing fundamentally wrong with the business and that with better management there could be considerable scope for improvement in return on capital employed and overall performance.

Task 2.2

a) The objective of financial statements is to provide information about the financial position, financial performance and changes in financial position of an entity that is useful to a wide range of users in making economic decisions. They also show the results of the stewardship of management, or the accountability of management for the resources entrusted to it. Users need to assess the stewardship of management in order to make economic decisions.

In the previous task, an investor and his advisor were using ratios based on financial statements to assess the stewardship of management (how well the directors had managed the business in the past year) and the overall financial performance of the company. The investor may use this information to decide whether to hold or sell his investment in the company or possibly (if he has a major shareholding or can combine with other investors) to decide whether the directors should be reappointed or replaced.

b) Other users of financial statements include:

Employees

Employees are interested in information about the stability and profitability of their employers. They are also interested in information that helps them to assess their employer's ability to provide wages, salaries and other benefits and employment opportunities.

Lenders

Lenders are interested in information that helps them to assess whether their loans and the interest attaching to them will be paid when due.

PRACTICE EXAM 2

TRUSTDAN PLC

ANSWERS

SECTION 1

PART A

Task 1.1

Trustdan plc
Consolidated balance sheet as at 31 March 20X6

	£'000
Non-current assets	
Goodwill (W1)	3,958
Property, plant and equipment (75,107 + 32,637 + 3,000)	110,744
	114,702
Current assets	
Inventories (28,273 + 7,663)	35,936
Trade and other receivables (11,508 + 5,154)	16,662
Cash and cash equivalents (2,146 + 68)	2,214
	54,812
Total assets	169,514
Current liabilities	
Trade and other payables (14,854 + 2,914)	(17,768)
Tax liabilities (6,230 + 108)	(6,338)
	(24,106)
Net current assets	30,706
Non-current liabilities	
Long-term loan (40,000 + 5,000)	(45,000)
Total liabilities	(69,106)
Net assets	100,408
EQUITY	
Share capital	35,000
Share premium	15,000
Retained earnings (W2)	41,033
Equity attributable to equity holders of the parent	91,033
Minority interest (W3)	9,375
Total equity	100,408

Tutorial note: Make sure that you did not include in your balance sheet the balances owing between Trustdan and Isold. These are intra-group receivables and payables and as such they are cancelled on consolidation.

Workings

Working 1 – Goodwill

	£'000	£'000
Purchase consideration		28,000
Net assets acquired:		
Share capital	10,000	
Share premium	2,000	
Retained earnings	17,056	
Fair value adjustment	3,000	
	32,056	
Group share 7,500,000/1,000,000 = 75% x 32,056		24,042
Goodwill		3,958

Working 2 – Consolidated retained earnings

	£'000
Trustdan	36,950
Isold – group share of post acquisition retained earnings	
(22,500 – 17,056) x 75%	4,083
	41,033

Working 3 –Minority interest

	£'000
Minority share of balance sheet value 25% x 34,500	8,625
Minority share of fair value adjustment 25% x 3,000	750
	9,375

Task 1.2

a) A business combination arises where two or more entities combine into one reporting entity. This is actually defined in IFRS 3 as "the bringing together of separate entities or businesses into one reporting entity".

b) The acquirer in a business combination is identified by determining which of the entities in the combination gains "control" of the other entity/entities. The acquirer is defined in IFRS 3 as "the combining entity that obtains control of the other combining entities or businesses".

c) One of the ways in which an entity can gain control of another is if it acquired more than half of the voting rights of the other entity. In this case Trustdan plc purchases 75% of the shares of Isold Ltd which carry 75% of the voting rights. Therefore Trustdan plc acquires control of Isold Ltd.

Tutorial note: For a good answer you needed to introduce the concept of control as well as owning at least half of the voting rights.

Part B

Task 1.3

			£'000	£'000
1	DR	Sales	3,147	
	CR	Trade receivables		3,147
2	DR	Inventory (Balance sheet)	8,107	
	CR	Inventory (Income statement)		8,107
3	DR	Distribution costs	157	
	CR	Accruals		157
4	DR	Interest	200	
	CR	Interest payable		200
5	DR	Taxation	235	
	CR	Taxation payable		235

Examiner's comments: The examiner felt that many candidates did not read the original journals carefully enough and therefore missed out on the some of the errors, either in which accounts were being debited and credited or in the numbers being used.

Task 1.4

a) **Tanhosier Ltd**
Income statement for the year ended 31 March 20X6

	£'000
Continuing operations	
Revenue (50,332 – 3,147)	47,185
Cost of sales (W)	(29,536)
Gross profit	17,649
Distribution costs (8,985 + 157)	(9,142)
Administrative expenses	(7,039)
Profit from operations	1,468
Finance costs (5,000 x 8%)	(400)
Profit before tax	1,068
Tax	(235)
Profit for the period from continuing operations attributable to equity holders	833

Tutorial note: Do not be put off by the pro forma in the answer booklet (included in the exam on the AAT's website, but not in this book) which includes a line for discontinued operations. This would appear to be a red herring and there are clearly no discontinued operations in this scenario.

Working

Cost of sales

	£'000
Opening inventory	7,865
Purchases	29,778
Less: closing inventory (8,407 – 300)	(8,107)
Cost of sales	29,536

b) **Tanhosier Ltd**
Balance sheet as at 31 March 20X6

	£'000
Non-current assets	
Property, plant and equipment (59,088 – 25,486)	33,602
Current assets	
Inventories (8,407 – 300)	8,107
Trade receivables (9,045 – 3,147)	5,898
Cash and cash equivalents	182
	14,187
Total assets	47,789
Current liabilities	
Trade and other payables (W)	(3,264)
Tax liabilities	(235)
	(3,499)
Net current assets	10,688
Non-current liabilities	
8% bank loan	(5,000)
Total liabilities	(8,499)
Net assets	39,290
EQUITY	
Share capital	10,000
Share premium	5,000
Retained earnings (23,457 + 833)	24,290
Total equity	39,290

Working

Trade and other payables

	£'000
Trade payables	2,481
Accruals (426 + 157)	583
Interest payable	200
	3,264

Tutorial note: Make sure that when preparing the income statement and balance sheet you do incorporate the journals from the previous task.

Task 1.5

a) An intangible asset is an asset of the business which has no physical form. To give it its technical definition from IAS 38 it is "an identifiable non-monetary asset without physical substance".

b) An intangible asset arising from development costs is known as development expenditure and can only be recognised as an intangible asset in the balance sheet when the following criteria have been demonstrated:

    i)   the technical feasibility of completing the intangible asset so that it will be available for sale or use

    ii)   the intention to complete the intangible asset and use or sell it

    iii) the ability to use or sell the intangible asset

    iv) how the intangible asset will generate future economic benefits

    v)   the availability of adequate technical, financial and other resources to complete the development and to use or sell the intangible asset

    vi) the ability to measure reliably the expenditure attributable to the intangible asset during its development.

Examiner's comments: In part a) whereas many candidates appreciated that an intangible asset was something without physical substance few recognised that such assets are also non-monetary. In general the examiner felt that IAS 38 had not been well enough revised by candidates.

Part C

Task 1.6

Lowandgrim Ltd
Reconciliation of profit from operations to net cash from operating activities

	£'000
Profit from operations	4,214
Adjustments:	
Depreciation	4,555
Gain on disposal of property, plant and equipment	(274)
Operating cash flows before movements in working capital	8,495
Movements in working capital	
Increase in inventories	(432)
Increase in trade receivables	(270)
Increase in trade payables	377
Cash generated by operations	8,170
Interest paid	(480)
Income taxes paid	(662)
Net cash from operating activities	7,028

Tutorial note: There was no pro-forma provided in the answer booklet for this task therefore you need to remember what items appear in this reconciliation. It was not strictly necessary to include interest paid here as it is allowed by IAS 7 to include it in the cash flow statement itself. The income tax charge in the income statement is the same as the liability in the current balance sheet which tells you that the amount of tax paid during the year must have been last year's income tax liability from the balance sheet.

Task 1.7

Lowandgrim Ltd
Cash flow statement for the year ended 31 March 20X6

	£'000
Net cash from operating activities	7,028
Investing activities	
Proceeds from sale of property, plant and equipment (W1)	809
Purchases of property, plant and equipment (W2)	(13,430)
Net cash used in investing activities	(12,621)
Financing activities	
Bank loans raised (6,000 – 4,000)	2,000
Proceeds from share issue (W3)	4,000
Net cash from financing activities	6,000
Net increase in cash and cash equivalents	407
Cash and cash equivalents at beginning of year	81
Cash and cash equivalents at end of year	488

Workings

Working 1 – Proceeds from sale of property, plant and equipment

	£'000
Cost	1,022
Accumulated depreciation	(487)
Net book value	535
Gain on disposal	274
Proceeds from disposal	809

Working 2 – Purchases of property, plant and equipment

Property, plant and equipment at NBV

	£'000		£'000
Opening balance	30,370	Disposal (W1)	535
Additions (bal fig)	13,430	Depreciation	4,555
		Closing balance	38,710
	43,800		43,800

Tutorial note: Make sure that you fully understand this working for the calculation of purchases of non current assets as it will tend to appear in all cash flow statement questions.

Working 3 – Proceeds from share issue

	£'000
Increase in share capital (6,000 – 4,000)	2,000
Increase in share premium (3,000 – 1,000)	2,000
	4,000

SECTION 2

Task 2.1

REPORT

To: Rachel Wagnor   Date: June 20X6
From: Accounting Technician   Subject: Wring Ltd

As requested this report assesses the efficiency and effectiveness of the management of Wring Ltd for the two years ended 31 March 20X5 and 20X6.

(a) **Formulae for calculating ratios**

Gross profit ratio $= \dfrac{\text{Gross profit}}{\text{Revenue}} \times 100$

Net profit ratio $= \dfrac{\text{Profit from operations}}{\text{Revenue}} \times 100$

Inventories turnover $= \dfrac{\text{Inventories}}{\text{Cost of sales}} \times 100$

Trade receivables turnover $= \dfrac{\text{Trade receivables}}{\text{Revenue}} \times 100$

Examiner's comments: A significant number of candidates used an incorrect profit figure for the net profit ratio – using either profit before tax or profit after tax rather than profit before finance costs.

(b) **Calculation of ratios**

	20X6	20X5
Gross profit ratio	$\dfrac{11,595}{21,473} \times 100 = 54\%$	$\dfrac{10,339}{19,882} \times 100 = 52\%$
Net profit ratio	$\dfrac{4,080}{21,473} \times 100 = 19\%$	$\dfrac{4,374}{19,882} \times 100 = 22\%$
Inventories turnover days	$\dfrac{1,813}{9,878} \times 365 = 67$ days	$\dfrac{1,438}{9,543} \times 365 = 55$
Trade receivables turnover days	$\dfrac{3,000}{21,473} \times 365 = 51$ days	$\dfrac{1,906}{19,882} \times 365 = 35$

c) **Comment on performance**

Gross profit ratio

The gross profit ratio measures the profit made from the actual trading activities of the company and would normally be expected to remain fairly constant. For Wring Ltd there has been an increase over the two year period from 52% to 54% which indicates that more profit is being made from trading. This could be due to an increase in prices or a reduction in cost of sales or a combination of the two.

Net profit ratio

As the gross profit margin has increased over the two years one would hope to see a similar increase in net profit ratio. However in this case there has been a decrease in net profit margin from 22% to 19%. This is due to an increase in expenses which has not only cancelled out the improved gross profit margin but also led to a decrease in overall profit. In fact if the expenses are taken as a percentage of revenue they have increased from 30% in 20X5 to 35% in 20X6.

Inventories turnover

The inventories turnover has increased from 55 days to 67 days over the two year period. This means that inventory is being held for 12 days longer than last year before it is sold. This could be a function of the increase in revenue which demands a higher inventory holding or could be an indication of poor working capital management.

Trade receivables turnover

The trade receivables turnover has increased from 35 days in 20X5 to 51 days in 20X6. This means that on average it is now taking 16 days longer to collect the amounts due from trade receivables. It is possible that this is a positive policy from management who are giving more generous credit terms in order to increase revenue. Alternatively this could be evidence of poor credit control procedures.

d) **Suggestions concerning improvement in performance**

Gross profit

The gross profit ratio could be improved even further either by increasing the selling price of the goods without incurring any additional cost of sales or by reducing cost of sales for example by seeking bulk discounts from suppliers.

Net profit

The net profit ratio could be improved by a reduction in the expenses of the business. Although the distribution costs have remained at a constant percentage of sales revenue the administration expenses have increased from 10.5% of revenue to 15.5%. Therefore management should concentrate on control and reduction of these administration expenses.

Inventories turnover

The inventories turnover ratio could be improved by reducing the amount of inventories held ready for sale. This could be done by increased control of the warehouse and the ordering and purchasing/manufacturing of goods. The increased turnover period may indicate that there are slow-moving items of inventory which may need to be written off due to obsolescence.

Trade receivables turnover

The length of time that it takes for credit customers to pay the amounts due can be reduced by improved credit control procedures. The terms of sale should be made clear to credit customers and any overdue debts followed up and collected.

I hope this information has been of use. If I can help further please do not hesitate to contact me.

Task 2.2

a) The accounting equation is: Assets – Liabilities = Equity

Each of these elements is defined in the IASB's Framework for the Preparation and Presentation of Financial Statements as follows:

"An asset is a resource controlled by an entity as a result of past events and from which future economic benefits are expected to flow to the entity".

"A liability is a present obligation arising from past events, the settlement of which is expected to result in the outflow from the entity of resources embodying economic benefits".

"Equity is the residual interest in the assets of the entity after deducting all its liabilities".

Tutorial note: These definitions, particularly those of assets and liabilities, are of fundamental importance to all accounting matters. It is not necessary to memorise these definitions but make sure that you can remember the essence of them.

b) A profit comes from income exceeding expenses. Income is generally an increase in the assets of the entity and expenses are an increase in the liabilities. If a profit has been made then the net assets of the entity (assets – liabilities) will increase. This same profit is an increase in the equity of the entity as it accrues to the owners of the entity.

Examiner's comments: Although many were able to explain how profit affected equity, few were able to explain the effect on net assets (assets – liabilities).

PRACTICE EXAM 3

HOWARDSEND LTD

ANSWERS

SECTION 1

PART A

Task 1.1

		£'000	£'000
1	Dr Purchases	2,403	
	Cr Trade payables		2,403
2	Dr Administrative expenses	79	
	Cr Allowance for doubtful receivables (2% x 6,600 – 53)		79
3	Dr Inventories (Balance Sheet)	8,134	
	Cr Inventories (Income Statement)		8,134
4	Dr Distribution costs	57	
	Cr Accruals		57
5	Dr Interest expense (7% x 10,000 x 6/12)	350	
	Cr Interest payable		350
6	Dr Tax expense	1,382	
	Cr Tax liabilities		1,382
7	Dr Property, plant and equipment	2,000	
	Cr Revaluation reserve (11,600 – 9,600)		2,000

Task 1.2

a) **Howardsend Ltd**
Income statement for the year ended 30 September 20X6

	£'000
Continuing operations	
Revenue (54,177 − 356)	53,821
Cost of sales (W1)	(25,834)
Gross profit	27,987
Distribution costs (12,216 + 57)	(12,273)
Administrative expenses (9,176 + 79)	(9,255)
Profit from operations	6,459
Finance costs (7% x 10,000)	(700)
Profit before tax	5,759
Tax	(1,382)
Profit for the period from continuing operations attributable to equity holders	4,377

b) **Howardsend Ltd**
Balance sheet as at 30 September 20X6

	£'000
Non-current assets	
Property, plant and equipment (W2)	44,626
Current assets	
Inventories	8,134
Trade receivables (W3)	6,468
Cash and cash equivalents	579
	15,181
Total assets	59,807
Current liabilities	
Trade and other payables (W4)	(5,601)
Tax liabilities	(1,382)
	(6,983)
Net current assets	8,198
Non-current liabilities	
Long-term loan	(10,000)
Total liabilities	(16,983)
Net assets	42,824
Equity	
Share capital	8,000
Share premium	1,000
Revaluation reserve	2,000
Retained earnings (W5)	31,824
Total equity	42,824

Workings

	£'000
1 *Cost of sales*	
Opening inventories	7,158
Purchases (24,610 + 2,403)	27,013
Returns outwards	(203)
Closing inventories	(8,134)
	25,834
2 *Property, plant and equipment*	
Cost	57,149
Accumulated depreciation	(14,523)
Revaluation (11,600 – 9,600)	2,000
	44,626

		£'000
3	*Trade receivables*	
	Trade receivables	6,600
	Less: allowance for doubtful receivables (2% x 6,600)	(132)
		6,468
4	*Trade and other payables*	
	Trade payables (2,577 + 2,403)	4,980
	Accruals	214
	Advertising	57
	Interest (7% x 10,000 x 6/12)	350
		5,601
5	*Retained earnings*	
	At 1 October 20X5	28,887
	Profit for the year	4,377
	Dividends paid (960 + 480)	(1,440)
		31,824

Tutorial note: Remember to deduct dividends paid during the year from retained earnings.

c) A professional accountant has a duty to maintain confidentiality when preparing financial statements for an employer or a client. This means that he or she should not pass information about a client's or an employer's business or other affairs to third parties unless authorised to do so or (in very rare circumstances) there is a legal obligation to do so. In particular, information should not be used for personal advantage or the advantage of a third party, such as an investor or a competitor.

Examiner's comments: The Chief Assessor commented that weaker students sometimes just explained the need for confidentiality without giving any examples of how this was assured.

Part B

Task 1.3

Goodwill

	£'000	£'000
Cost of investment		29,000
Less: fair value of net assets acquired:		
Share capital	5,000	
Share premium	2,000	
Retained earnings	24,700	
Fair value adjustment (37,000 – 33,000)	4,000	
	35,700	
Group share (60%)		(21,420)
		7,580
Less: impairment loss (20% x 7,580)		(1,516)
		6,064

Minority interest

	£'000
Net assets at balance sheet date	35,370
Fair value adjustment	4,000
	39,370
Minority interest share (40%)	15,748

Consolidated retained earnings

	£'000	£'000
Klarke plc		34,225
Cameroon Ltd:		
At balance sheet date	28,370	
At acquisition	(24,700)	
	3,670	
Group share (60%)		2,202
		36,427
Less: impairment loss (20% x 7,580)		(1,516)
		34,911

Working

Group structure

Klarke plc owns 60% of Cameroon Ltd (3,000,000/5,000,000)

Task 1.4

a) The carrying value of an asset is the cost of an asset less accumulated depreciation and accumulated impairment losses. It is the amount at which an asset is recognised in the balance sheet.

The recoverable amount of an asset is the higher of an asset's fair value less costs to sell and its value in use. Value in use is the present value of the future cash flows expected to be derived from an asset.

b) If the recoverable amount of an asset falls below its carrying amount, it is impaired. The impairment loss is the difference between the asset's carrying amount and its recoverable amount.

c) An impairment loss is normally recognised immediately in the income statement as an expense. However, if the asset has previously been revalued upwards, the loss is offset against the revaluation surplus relating to the asset. If the loss is greater than the revaluation surplus relating to the asset, the excess is recognised in the income statement.

PART C

Task 1.5

Reconciliation of profit from operations to net cash from operating activities

	£'000
Profit from operations	5,630
Adjustments for:	
Depreciation	2,172
Loss on disposal of property, plant and equipment	183
Operating cash flows before movements in working capital	7,985
Increase in inventories (4,837 – 4,502)	(335)
Increase in trade receivables (5,244 – 4,978)	(266)
Increase in trade payables (3,038 – 2,954)	84
Cash generated from operations	7,468
Income taxes paid	(854)
Interest paid	(800)
Net cash from operating activities	5,814

Task 1.6

Kenadie Ltd
Cash flow statement for the year ended 30 September 20X6

	£'000	£'000
Net cash from operating activities		5,814
Investing activities		
Purchases of property, plant and equipment (W2)	(13,646)	
Proceeds from sale of property, plant and equipment (W1)	509	
Net cash used in investing activities		(13,137)
Financing activities		
Proceeds from issue of share capital (10,500 – 6,000)	4,500	
Increase in bank loans (10,000 – 7,000)	3,000	
Dividends paid	(700)	
Net cash from financing activities		6,800
Net decrease in cash and cash equivalents		(523)
Cash and cash equivalents at the beginning of the year		587
Cash and cash equivalents at the end of the year		64

Workings

1   Property, plant and equipment

	£'000		£'000
Balance b/d	19,100	Depreciation	2,172
Additions (balancing figure)	13,646	Disposals (1,103 – 411)	692
		Balance c/d	29,882
	32,746		32,746

2   Proceeds from sale of property, plant and equipment

	£'000
Cost	1,103
Accumulated depreciation	(411)
Net book value	692
Loss	(183)
Cash received	509

SECTION 2

Task 2.1

Name
Address
Date

Dear Ms Tair,

Profitability and effectiveness of Labor Ltd

As requested, I have analysed the financial statements of Labor Ltd for the two years ended 30 September 20X5 and 30 September 20X6. I have based my analysis on four key ratios: return on capital employed; net profit ratio; gross profit ratio; and asset turnover. I explain the calculation and significance of these and set out my further comments below.

Formulae used to calculate the ratios

i) Return on capital employed
$$\frac{\text{Profit from operations}}{\text{Capital employed}}$$

ii) Net profit ratio
$$\frac{\text{Profit from operations}}{\text{Sales}}$$

iii) Gross profit ratio
$$\frac{\text{Gross profit}}{\text{Sales}}$$

iv) Asset turnover
$$\frac{\text{Sales}}{\text{Capital employed}}$$

Calculation of the ratios

		20X6	20X5
i)	Return on capital employed	$\frac{3,626}{27,679} \times 100\% = 13.1\%$	$\frac{4,477}{29,379} \times 100\% = 15.2\%$
ii)	Net profit ratio	$\frac{3,626}{37,384} \times 100\% = 9.7\%$	$\frac{4,477}{36,103} \times 100\% = 12.4\%$
iii)	Gross profit ratio	$\frac{15,926}{37,384} \times 100\% = 42.6\%$	$\frac{14,983}{36,103} \times 100\% = 41.5\%$
iv)	Asset turnover	$\frac{37,384}{27,679} = 1.35$ times	$\frac{36,103}{29,379} = 1.23$ times

The performance and effectiveness of the company

Return on capital employed

This ratio measures the overall performance of the company by showing the profit generated as a percentage of the capital employed by the company. Capital employed is the shareholders' equity (share capital and reserves) plus long-term debt. Return on capital employed has fallen in 20X6, which mean that the company is generating a lower return for each £ of capital employed in the company' operations. This means that either the company is less profitable or that it is using its resources les efficiently than before.

Net profit ratio

This ratio measures the net profit, or profit from operations, as a percentage of the company's sales. I has fallen from 12.7% in 20X5 to 9.7% in 20X6. The reason for the fall appears to be that botl distribution costs and administrative expenses have risen in 20X6. Administrative expenses have increased by 35% and operating expenses have risen to 33% of sales compared with 29% in 20X5.

Gross profit ratio

This ratio measures the gross profit as a percentage of sales, or gross profit margin. This has risen slightl during the period, which shows that the margin on sales is not the reason for the deterioration in the ne profit margin. Gross profit has also risen in absolute terms. The reason for the improvement may be a increase in sales prices or a reduction in cost of sales or both.

Asset turnover

This ratio compares sales revenue with the capital employed in the business. It shows how efficiently the company has used its resources to generate sales. Asset turnover has increased from 1.23 times to 1.3 times in the period, which means that the company is using its assets more effectively than before.

The overall change in financial performance and effectiveness

The company's return on capital employed has deteriorated in 20X6, which means that it is generatin less profit from the capital used in the business. Sales have increased slightly and the gross profit margi has improved. In addition, the company appears to be using its capital more effectively to generate sales However, the additional gross profit has been absorbed by an increase in distribution costs and administrative expenses. This means that net profit margins have fallen and that overall, the company i less profitable in 20X6.

I hope that this information has been helpful. If you have any further questions, or require any furthe assistance, please do not hesitate to contact me.

Yours sincerely,

Signature

Tutorial note: To perform this task well, you needed to remember the way in which the ratios are linke to each other. Return on capital employed is the product of two of the three other ratios that you wer asked to calculate: ROCE = net profit margin x asset turnover. It can be divided into two elements profitability and use of assets.

Task 2.2

a) The Framework for the Preparation and Presentation of Financial Statements lists five elements of financial statements:

-   assets
-   liabilities
-   equity
-   income
-   expenses

b) Assets, liabilities and equity appear in the balance sheet of a company.

Assets are resources controlled by an entity as a result of past events and from which future economic benefits are expected to flow to the entity.

Liabilities are present obligations of an entity arising from past events, the settlement of which is expected to result in an outflow from the entity of resources embodying economic benefits.

Equity is the residual interest in the assets of an entity after deducting all its liabilities.

PRACTICE EXAM 4

RICSCHTEIN LTD

ANSWERS

SECTION 1

PART A

Task 1.1

Journal entries

			£'000	£'000
1	Dr	Cash (3,000 x £3)	9,000	
	Cr	Share capital (3,000 x £1)		3,000
	Cr	Share premium		6,000
2	Dr	Inventories (Balance Sheet)	7,304	
	Cr	Inventories (Income Statement)		7,304
3	Dr	Administrative expenses	87	
	Cr	Trade and other payables		87
4	Dr	Prepayments (36 x 3/12)	9	
	Cr	Administrative expenses		9
5	Dr	Interest (14,000 x 7% x 6/12)	490	
	Cr	Trade and other payables		490
6	Dr	Tax expense	1,170	
	Cr	Tax payable		1,170

Task 1.2

a)

Ricschtein Ltd
Company income statement for the year ended 31 March 20X7

	£'000
Continuing operations	
Revenue (37,365 – 641)	36,724
Cost of sales (W)	(20,565)
Gross profit	16,159
Distribution costs	(5,517)
Administrative expenses (3,904 + 87 – 9)	(3,982)
Profit from operations	6,660
Finance costs (490 + 490)	(980)
Profit before tax	5,680
Tax	(1,170)
Profit for the period from continuing operations	4,510
Discontinued operations	
Loss for the period from discontinued operations	(347)
Profit for the period attributable to equity holders	4,163

Workings

	£'000
Cost of sales	
Opening inventory	6,120
Purchases	22,157
Returns outwards	(408)
Closing inventory	(7,304)
	20,565

b)

Ricschtein Ltd
Company balance sheet at 31 March 20X7

	£'000
Non-current assets:	
Property, plant and equipment (39,371 – 13,892)	25,479
Current assets:	
Inventories	7,304
Trade receivables (4,590 + 9)	4,599
Cash and cash equivalents (423 + 9,000)	9,423
	21,326
Total assets	46,805
Current liabilities:	
Trade payables (2,236 + 87 + 490 + 207)	3,020
Tax payable	1,170
	4,190
Net current assets	17,136
Non-current liabilities:	
Bank loan	14,000
Total liabilities	18,190
Net assets	28,615
Equity:	
Share capital (7,000 + 3,000)	10,000
Share premium	6,000
Retained earnings (9,552 + 4,163 – 1,100)	12,615
Total equity	28,615

Task 1.3

a) Inventories are assets held by an entity that are for sale in the ordinary course of business. As Ricschtein Ltd purchases goods for resale, inventories held would be finished goods.

IAS 2 *Inventories* requires inventories to be recognised in the financial statements at the lower of cost and net realisable value.

The cost of inventory should include the purchase price, import duties and other taxes, and transport, handling and other costs directly attributable to the acquisition of the finished goods. Essentially, all costs incurred in bringing the inventory to its present location and condition can be included.

b) IAS 18 *Revenue* defines revenue as the 'gross inflows of economic benefits received and receivable by the entity on its own account'. In Ricschtein Ltd, revenue will arise from the sale of goods. IAS 18 states that revenue should be measured at the 'fair value of the consideration received or receivable'.

Revenue from the sale of goods shall be recognised when the following conditions have been satisfied:

i) The entity has transferred to the buyer the significant risks and rewards of ownership of the goods;

ii) The entity retains neither continuing managerial involvement nor effective control over the goods sold;

iii) The amount of revenue can be measured reliably;

iv) It is probable that economic benefits associated with the transaction will flow to the entity; and

v) The costs incurred or to be incurred in respect of the transaction can be measured reliably.

Part B

Task 1.4

Wraymand plc
Consolidated income statement for the year ended 31 March 20X7

	£'000
Continuing operations	
Revenue (38,462 + 12,544 - 1,600)	49,406
Cost of sales (22,693 + 5,268 - 1,600)	(26,361)
Gross profit	23,045
Distribution costs (6,403 + 2,851)	(9,254)
Administrative expenses (3,987 + 2,466)	(6,453)
Profit from operations	7,338
Finance costs (562 + 180)	(742)
Profit before tax	6,596
Tax (1,511 + 623)	(2,134)
Profit for the period from continuing operations	4,462
Attributable to:	
Equity holders of the parent	4,173
Minority interest (25% x 1,156)	289
	4,462

Task 1.5

Goramsee Ltd
Company cash flow statement for the year ended 31 March 20X7

	£'000
Net cash from operating activities	6,680
Investing activities	
Proceeds of sale of property, plant and equipment (W1)	740
Purchase of property, plant and equipment (W2)	(13,996)
Net cash used in investing activities	(13,256)
Financing activities	
Proceeds of new bank loans (8,000 - 6,000)	2,000
Proceeds of share issue (13,000 - 9,000)	4,000
Dividends paid	(960)
Net cash (used in)/from investing activities	5,040
Net increase/(decrease) in cash and cash equivalents	(1,536)
Cash and cash equivalents at the beginning of year	539
Cash and cash equivalents at end of year	(997)

Workings

1   *Proceeds of sale of PPE*

	£'000
Net book value at disposal (1,037 - 731)	306
Profit on sale	434
Proceeds	740

2   *Purchase of property, plant and equipment*

PPE – NBV

	£'000		£'000
b/f	26,084	Depreciation	4,217
Purchase (bal fig)	13,996	Disposals (W1)	306
		C/F	35,557
	40,080		40,080

Task 1.6

REPORT

To: Directors of Goramsee Ltd
From: Accountant
Date: June 20X7
Subject: Comments on operating cashflow of Goramsee Ltd

The income statement shows an increase in profit from operations in 20X7, although this increase does not continue into cash from operations, which has fallen slightly in the year. There are a number of reasons why the cash from operations has fallen.

- There has been a significant cash outflow relating to inventories. The inventory balance in the balance sheet has increased suggesting that control over inventory levels has weakened in the year. It may be a deliberate policy by management to ensure that there is sufficient inventory available, but it could also indicate slow moving or obsolete inventory.

- Trade receivables have also increased in the year which suggests that credit control policies have worsened. It is important that customers pay on time to avoid any bad debts occurring. Both the negative movement in receivables and inventory have reduced operating cashflow by £2 million.

- Trade payables have decreased slightly which suggests that creditors have been paid too quickly. It would appear that Goramsee Ltd are paying suppliers before receiving cash from customers. It would improve cashflow if they could delay payments to suppliers.

- There has been a slight increase in interest and tax paid during the year but this has not had a significant effect on cashflow.

The key reason for the reduction in operating cash flow is the poor control of working capital. This needs addressing urgently as it has already caused a positive cash balance to become an overdraft and the company needs to halt any further deterioration of its cash position.

SECTION 2

Task 2.1

Accounting Technician
20 High Street
Anytown

20 June 20X7

Dear Sir,

As requested, I have reviewed the financial statements of Gariroads Ltd to establish whether further finance could be obtained for expansion.

Based on the financial statements for the year ended 31 March 20X6 and 20X7, I have calculated the following ratios.

				20X7	20X6
a)	i)	Current ratio	$\dfrac{\text{Current assets}}{\text{Current liabilities}}$	$\dfrac{6,337}{2,906} = 2.2$	$\dfrac{6,197}{2,951} = 2.1$
	ii)	Quick ratio	$\dfrac{\text{Current assets - inventories}}{\text{Current liabilities}}$	$\dfrac{2,325}{2,906} = 0.8$	$\dfrac{3,734}{2,951} = 1.3$
	iii)	Gearing ratio	$\dfrac{\text{Long - term debt}}{\text{Equity + debt}}$	$\dfrac{14,000}{27,413} = 51.1\%$	$\dfrac{6,000}{19,261} = 31.2\%$
	iv)	Interest cover	$\dfrac{\text{Profit before interest + tax}}{\text{Interest cost}}$	$\dfrac{1,405}{800} = 1.8$ times	$\dfrac{2,182}{480} = 4.5$ times

b) *Explanation of the meaning of the ratios*

The current ratio shows the extent to which the company's current liabilities are covered by its current assets. It is an important measure of liquidity as a ratio that is very low suggests a company would have difficulty in paying liabilities as they fall due. Alternatively, a very high ratio suggests inefficiency as too much cash is invested in current assets.

The quick or acid test ratio shows the extent to which a company can meet its day to day liabilities from its cash and receivables balances only. Inventory is excluded from the calculation as it is the least liquid of the current assets.

The gearing ratio measures the level of a company's debt in comparison to capital employed. The higher the ratio, the more risky a company is deemed to be. This is because if profits fall, interest on loans must still be paid and this reduces the amounts available to pay as a dividend to the ordinary shareholders.

The interest cover ratio shows how many times a company can meet its interest payments out of the current year profits. The higher the cover, the more secure the interest payments which would satisfy lenders. A low level of interest cost may mean that if profits fall, the company may struggle to meet its interest payments.

c)   *Commentary on liquidity and financial position*

There has been a slight increase in the current ratio in the year which is positive and the overall ratio is at a comfortable level above 2. However, the quick ratio shows a worsening position as it has fallen from 1.3 to 0.8 showing that Gariroads may struggle to meet its obligations from assets that are quickly convertible into cash. The reason for the fall in the ratio is the increased inventory which has had a negative effect on the cash balance.

The gearing ratio has increased in the year from a relatively safe 31% to a high 51%. New loans have been taken out during the year and the company is likely to be seen as risky by future lenders.

Interest cover has decreased from 4.5 times to 1.8 times which again would be seen as a risk factor by lenders. There are less profits available to cover the interest payments so future lenders would be very cautious about lending money to Gariroads Ltd.

d)   *Conclusion*

Overall, Gariroads has a worsening liquidity position and increased gearing in 20X7 compared to 20X6. Whilst the company is still able to meet its interest payments, the ability to do so has decreased.

All of these factors combined mean that Gariroads Ltd is less attractive to lenders and based on the four ratios calculated, it is unlikely that the bank would lend further cash to the business at the moment. Gariroads Ltd may wish to consider raising equity finance as an alternative.

Yours faithfully

Accounting Technician

Task 2.2

a)   The IASB Framework for the Preparation and Presentation of Financial Statements states that the objective of financial statements is to provide information about the financial position, performance and changes in financial position of an entity that is useful to a wide range of users in making economic decisions.

b)   Users of the financial statements include the following:

i)   *Investors*. They need information to help determine whether they should buy, hold or sell their shares. They also need information that enables them to assess the ability of the entity to pay dividends.

ii)   *Employees*. They are interested in the stability and profitability of their employer. They also need information to assess the ability of their employer to provide remuneration, retirement benefits and employment opportunities.

iii) *Lenders*. They are interested in whether their loans and the interest attaching to them will be paid when due.

iv)   *Suppliers and other trade creditors*. They are interested in whether amounts owing to them will be paid when due.

v)   *Customers*. They are interested in the continuance of an entity, especially when they have a long term involvement with, or are dependent on, the entity.

vi)   *Governments and their agencies*. They are interested in the allocation of resources and therefore the activities of entities. Information may be used to regulate entities, determine taxation policies and for statistical purposes.

vii) *Public*. They may be interested in the trends and recent developments in the prosperity of the entity and the range of its activities.

[Note. The question only required the discussion of two of the users listed above.]

PRACTICE EXAM 5

BENARD LTD

ANSWERS

SECTION 1

PART A

Task 1.1

Journal entries

		£'000 Dr	£'000 Cr
Dr	Trade receivables	3,564	
Cr	Sales		3,564
Dr	Inventory (Balance Sheet)	9,786	
Dr	Inventory (Income Statement)		9,786
Dr	Trade payables	127	
Cr	Returns outwards		127
Dr	Prepayments (48,000 x 8/12)	32	
Cr	Administrative expenses		32
Dr	Interest	560	
Cr	Accruals (16,000 x 7% x 6/12)		560
Dr	Tax expense	1,254	
Cr	Tax payable		1,254

Task 1.2

a)   **Benard Ltd**
     Company income statement for the year ended 31 October 20X7

	£'000
Continuing operations	
Revenue (50,875 + 3,564 - 678)	53,761
Cost of sales (W)	(33,335)
Gross profit	20,426
Distribution costs	(6,654)
Administrative expenses (4,152 - 32)	(4,120)
Profit from operations	9,652
Finance costs (560 + 560)	(1,120)
Profit before tax	8,532
Tax	(1,254)
Profit for the period attributable to equity holders	7,278

Working

	£'000
Cost of sales	
Opening inventory	8,456
Purchases	35,245
Returns outwards (453 + 127)	(580)
Closing inventory	(9,786)
	33,335

b) **Benard Ltd**
Company balance sheet as at 31 October 20X7

	£'000
Non-current assets	
Property, plant and equipment (58,463 - 27,974)	30,489
Current assets	
Inventories	9,786
Trade and other receivables (6,690 + 3,564 + 32)	10,286
Cash and cash equivalents	1,184
	21,256
Total assets	51,745
Current liabilities	
Trade and other payables (3,348 + 387 - 127 + 560)	4,168
Tax payable	1,254
	5,422
Net current assets	15,834
Non-current liabilities	
Bank loan	16,000
Total liabilities	21,422
Net assets	30,323
Equity	
Share capital	12,000
Retained earnings (W1)	18,323
Total equity	30,323

Working

	£'000
Retained earnings	
b/f	12,345
Profit for year	7,278
Dividends: interim	(600)
final	(700)
	18,323

Part B

Task 1.3

Dumyat plc
Consolidated balance sheet at 31 October 20X7

	£'000
Non-current assets:	
Goodwill (W1)	2,711
Property, plant and equipment (65,388 + 31,887 + 3,000)	100,275
	102,986
Current assets:	
Inventories (28,273 + 5,566)	33,839
Trade and other receivables (11,508 + 5,154)	16,662
Cash and cash equivalents (2,146 + 68)	2,214
	52,715
Total assets	155,701
Current liabilities:	
Trade and other payables (13,554 + 1,475)	15,029
Tax payable (6,140 + 108)	6,248
	21,277
Net current assets	31,438
Non-current liabilities:	
Long-term loans (25,000 + 4,000)	29,000
Total liabilities	50,277
Net assets	105,424
Equity	
Share capital	25,000
Share premium	12,000
Retained earnings (W2)	59,401
Equity attributable to equity holders of the parent	96,401
Minority interest (W3)	9,023
Total equity	105,424

Workings

1 *Goodwill*

	£'000	£'000
Cost of investment		26,000
Less: net assets acquired:		
Share capital	12,000	
Share premium	4,000	
Retained earnings	12,052	
Fair value adjustment (28,800 - 25,800)	3,000	
	31,052	
Group share 75%		(23,289)
Goodwill		2,711

2 *Consolidated retained earnings reserve*

	£'000	£'000
Dumyat plc		55,621
Devon Ltd		
At balance sheet date	17,092	
At acquisition	(12,052)	
	5,040	
Group share 75%		3,780
		59,401

3 *Minority interest*

	£'000
Share capital	12,000
Share premium	4,000
Retained earnings	17,092
Fair value adjustment	3,000
	36,092
Minority share 25%	9,023

Task 1.4

a) IFRS 3 *Business combinations* defines a business combination as 'the bringing together of separate entities or businesses into one reporting entity'.

b) IFRS 3 defines the acquirer as 'the combining entity that obtains control of the other combining entities or businesses'.

c) Dumyat plc is the acquirer in this business combination as it has obtained control of Devon Ltd.

IFRS 3 defines control as 'the power to govern the financial and operating policies of an entity or business so as to obtain benefits from its activities'.

Control is presumed to have been obtained when one entity acquires more than one-half of that other entity's voting rights. As Dumyat plc acquired 75% of the ordinary share capital of Devon Ltd, this would give Dumyat plc control of Devon Ltd.

Task 1.5

Reconciliation of profit from operations to net cash from operating activities

	£'000
Profit from operations	3,360
Adjustments:	
Depreciation	3,545
Profit on sale of non-current assets	(224)
Operating cashflow before working capital movements	6,681
Increase in inventories (3,696 – 2,464)	(1,232)
Increase in trade receivables (3,360 – 2,464)	(896)
Decrease in trade payables (1,232 – 1,848)	(616)
Cash from operations	3,937
Interest paid	(91)
Tax paid	(944)
Net cash inflow from operating activities	2,902

Task 1.6

Lochnagar Ltd
Cash flow statement for the year ended 31 October 20X7

	£'000
Net cash from operating activities (Task 1.5)	2,902
Investing activities	
Proceeds of disposal of non-current assets (W1)	845
Purchase of non-current assets (W2)	(5,237)
Net cash used in investing activities	(4,392)
Financing activities	
Issue of share capital (3,000 – 2,500)	500
Cash received from bank loans (1,300 – 800)	500
Net cash (used in)/from financing activities	1,000
Net increase/(decrease) in cash and cash equivalents	(490)
Cash and cash equivalents at the beginning of year	129
Cash and cash equivalents at the end of year	(361)

Workings

1   *Proceeds of disposal of non-current assets*

	£'000
Carrying value at disposal (976 – 355)	621
Profit on disposal	224
Proceeds	845

2   *Purchase of non-current assets*

Non-current assets

	£'000		£'000
b/f	24,100	Depreciation	3,545
Additions (bal fig)	5,237	Disposals (W1)	621
		c/f	25,171
	29,337		29,337

SECTION 2

Task 2.1

REPORT

To: Sally Forth
From: Accounting Technician
Subject: Review of financial statements of Tay Ltd
Date: December 20X7

As requested, I have analysed the efficiency and effectiveness of the management of Tay Ltd. Using the financial statements for the financial years ended 31 October 20X7 and 20X6, I have calculated the following ratios.

a)   i)   Gross profit ratio $\dfrac{\text{Gross profit}}{\text{Revenue}} \times 100\%$

    ii)   Net profit ratio $\dfrac{\text{Profit from operations}}{\text{Revenue}} \times 100\%$

    iii)   Inventory turnover (days) $\dfrac{\text{Inventory}}{\text{Cost of sales}} \times 365$

    iv)   Trade receivables turnover $\dfrac{\text{Trade receivables}}{\text{Revenue}} \times 365$

b)   **Calculation of ratios**

		20X7	20X6
i)	Gross profit ratios	$\dfrac{1{,}008}{2{,}400} = 42\%$	$\dfrac{945}{2{,}100} = 45\%$
ii)	Net profit ratio	$\dfrac{228}{2{,}400} = 9.5\%$	$\dfrac{158}{2{,}100} = 7.5\%$
iii)	Inventory turnover	$\dfrac{320}{1{,}392} \times 365 = 83.9 \text{ days}$	$\dfrac{208}{1{,}155} \times 365 = 65.7 \text{ days}$
iv)	Trade receivables turnover	$\dfrac{360}{2{,}400} \times 365 = 54.8 \text{ days}$	$\dfrac{231}{2{,}100} \times 365 = 40.2 \text{ days}$

c) **Comments on performance**

Gross profit ratio
The gross profit ratio measures the level of profitability from the trading operation of the business. For Tay Ltd, the gross profit margin has fallen in 20X7, from 45% to 42%. There could be many reasons for a fall in profitability, for example, raw material prices may have increased and Tay Ltd have been unable to pass on these price increases to customers. Alternatively, management may have cut prices to try and attract new sales.

Net profit ratio
The net profit ratio has increased from 7.5% to 9.5% which is an improvement. As the gross margin has fallen, the increase in the net margin must be as a result of lower overhead costs. Tay Ltd has obviously had strong control of costs during the year.

Inventory turnover
The inventory turnover ratio measures the number of days inventory is held in the business. The shorter the holding period, the quicker the inventory is turned into cash. Tay Ltd's inventory turnover period has increased significantly from 65.7 days in 20X6 to 83.9 days in 20X7. This means Tay Ltd are less efficient in managing inventory in the current year.

Trade receivables turnover
The trade receivables turnover has also worsened, with debts being collected over 54.8 days in 20X7 compared to 40.2 days in 20X6. It could be that management have allowed more credit to customers or it may be a sign of worsening credit control or the possibility of bad debts.

d) **Suggestions for improvement of the ratios**

Gross profit
The gross profit ratio could be improved if selling prices could be increased without a corresponding increase in costs. Alternatively, raw materials or goods for resale could be sourced for lower prices.

Net profit
This ratio will improve if cost savings can be made. As administrative expenses have reduced in 20X7, it may be that reductions could be made in distribution costs.

Inventory turnover
The slow moving inventory may indicate old or obsolete inventory, so this may need to be written off. Management need to improve inventory ordering and purchasing/manufacture so that high levels of inventory are not held, tying up cash in the business.

Trade receivables turnover
As trade receivables turnover has increased, management should assess the recoverability of receivables. Credit control procedures should be tightened so that cash can be collected on a timely basis.

Task 2.2

a) The accounting equation is:

$$\text{Assets - Liabilities} = \text{Equity}$$

The elements in the accounting equation are defined in the IASB Framework for the Preparation and Presentation of Financial Statements, as follows:

'An asset is a resource controlled by an entity as a result of past events and from which future economic benefits are expected to flow to the entity.'

'A liability is a present obligation arising from past events, the settlement of which is expected to result in the outflow from the entity of resources embodying economic benefits.'

'Equity is the residual Interest in the assets of the entity after deducting all its liabilities.'

b) A profit arises when income exceeds expenses in the accounting period. If a profit has been made then the net assets of the entity will increase. The same profit also increases the equity of the entity as it accrues to the owners of the entity.

FORMS

We include here some blank proformas for your use when practising activities.

JOURNAL		
	Dr £'000	Cr £'000

COMPANY INCOME STATEMENT
FOR THE YEAR ENDED ....

£'000

Continuing operations

Revenue

Cost of sales

Gross profit

Distribution costs

Administrative expenses

Profit from operations

Finance costs

Profit before tax

Tax

Profit for the period from continuing operations

Discontinued operations

Loss for the period from discontinued operations

Profit for the period attributable to equity holders

COMPANY BALANCE SHEET
AT ....

£'000

Non-current assets

Current assets

Total assets

Current liabilities

Net current assets

Non-current liabilities

Total liabilities

Net assets

EQUITY

Total equity

CONSOLIDATED INCOME STATEMENT
FOR THE YEAR ENDED ....

£'000

Continuing operations

Revenue

Cost of sales

Gross profit

Distribution costs

Administrative expenses

Profit from operations

Finance costs

Profit before tax

Tax

Profit for the period from continuing operations

Discontinued operations

Loss for the period from discontinued operations

Profit for the period

Attributable to:

Equity holders of the parent

Minority interest

CONSOLIDATED STATEMENT OF RECOGNISED INCOME AND EXPENSE
FOR THE YEAR ENDED ……………………..

£'000

Net income recognised directly in equity

Transfers

Profit for the period

Total recognised income and expense for the period

Attributable to:

Equity holders of the parent

Minority interests

CONSOLIDATED BALANCE SHEET
AT ....

£'000

Non-current assets

Current assets

Total assets

Current liabilities

Net current assets

Non-current liabilities

Total liabilities

Net assets

EQUITY

Equity attributable to equity holders of the parent

Minority interest

Total equity

COMPANY CASH FLOW STATEMENT
FOR THE YEAR ENDED ....

£'000

Net cash from operating activities

Investing activities

Net cash used in investing activities

Financing activities

Net cash (used in)/from financing activities

Net increase/(decrease) in cash and cash equivalents

Cash and cash equivalents at beginning of year

Cash and cash equivalents at end of year